Social Determinants of Health

THE CANADIAN FACTS

2nd Edition

Dennis Raphael
Toba Bryant
Juha Mikkonen
Alexander Raphael

Social Determinants of Health: The Canadian Facts, 2nd Edition

Raphael, D., Bryant, T., Mikkonen, J. and Raphael, A. (2020). Social Determinants of Health: The Canadian Facts. Oshawa: Ontario Tech University Faculty of Health Sciences and Toronto: York University School of Health Policy and Management.

The publication is available at http://www.thecanadianfacts.org/

Cover Design by Alexander Raphael and Juha Mikkonen.

Cover photo: Double-crested cormorant (Phalacrocorax auritus) nesting at Tommy Thompson Park, Toronto.

Photographs by Alexander Raphael.

Formatting, Design and Content Organization by Juha Mikkonen.

Funding for this project was provided by Ontario Tech University Faculty of Health Sciences.

Library and Archives Canada Cataloguing in Publication

Social Determinants of Health: The Canadian Facts, 2nd Edition / Dennis Raphael, Toba Bryant, Juha Mikkonen and Alexander Raphael ISBN 978-0-9683484-2-0

1. Public health—Social aspects—Canada. 2. Public health—Economic aspects—Canada. 3. Medical policy—Social aspects—Canada. I. Raphael, Dennis, II. Bryant, Toba, III Mikkonen, Juha and IV Raphael, Alexander

Social Determinants of Health: The Canadian Facts (2nd Edition)

Authors and Contributors
Foreword to the Second Edition by Claire Betker, RN, PhD, CCHN(C)
Foreword to the First Edition by the Honourable Monique Bégin

This page intentionally left blank.

AUTHORS AND CONTRIBUTORS

Dennis Raphael, PhD (Toronto, Canada) is a Professor of Health Policy and Management at the School of Health Policy and Management at York University. He is the editor of Social Determinants of Health: Canadian Perspectives (2016, 3rd edition), Health Promotion and Quality of Life in Canada: Essential Readings (2010); Immigration, Public Policy, and Health: Newcomer Experiences in Developed Nations (2016) and Tackling Health Inequalities: Lessons from International Experiences (2012); co-editor of Staying Alive: Critical Perspectives on Health, Illness, and Health Care (2019, 3rd edition). He is author of About Canada: Health and Illness (2016, 2nd edition) and Poverty in Canada: Implications for Health and Quality of Life (2020, 3rd edition) and co-author with Toba Bryant of The Politics of Health in the Canadian Welfare State (2020). He manages the Social Determinants of Health Listserv at York University. Contact: draphael [at] yorku.ca

Toba Bryant, PhD (Toronto, Canada) is an Associate Professor, Faculty of Health Sciences, at Ontario Tech University in Oshawa, Ontario. She is author of Health Policy in Canada (2016, 2nd edition), and co-author with Dennis Raphael of The Politics of Health in the Canadian Welfare State. Dr. Bryant is co-editor of Staying Alive: Critical Perspectives on Health, Illness, and Health Care (2019, 3rd edition). She has published numerous book chapters and articles on policy change, housing as a social determinant of health, health within a population health perspective, the welfare state, health equity and community quality of life. Her most recent work is concerned with the effects of plant closures on the health and well-being of laid-off workers and their communities in Oshawa and how these communities are responding to these threats in an age of economic globalization. Contact: toba.bryant [at] uoit.ca

Juha Mikkonen, PhD (Helsinki, Finland) is a public policy professional and social psychologist with 18 years of professional experience. Dr. Mikkonen has held leadership positions in numerous non-profit organizations to promote health and well-being. He is Executive Director of the Finnish Association for Substance Abuse Prevention EHYT. He received his PhD in Health Policy and Equity from York University and a Master's Degree in Social Sciences from the University of Helsinki. Dr. Mikkonen is a practice-oriented expert in substance abuse prevention, health equity, intersectoral action, and the social determinants of health. Previously, as a consultant, Dr. Mikkonen provided expert advice to think tanks and international organizations including the World Health Organization. His public policy contributions include over 80 articles, books, reports, and professional presentations. Contact: mikkonen [at] iki.fi

Alexander Raphael (Toronto, Canada) is a third-year photography student in the Bachelor of Fine Arts Image Arts Program at Ryerson University in Toronto. Mr. Raphael has served as the official photographer for the Society for the Advancement of Science in Africa's 2019 Conference in Toronto and the 2018 Restructuring Work: A Discussion on the Topic of Labour and the Organization of Global Capitalism Conference in Oshawa. He has a professional photography practice in Toronto. Contact: alexraph62 [at] gmail.com

AUTHORS AND CONTRIBUTORS

Julia Fursova, PhD, Environmental Studies, is a Post-Doctoral Fellow in Evaluation, Faculty of Education, York University. Her doctoral research examined community action for health justice in urban environments with the focus on the role of non-profit organizations in advancing community participation. She contributed the section on **Geography**.

Morris DC Komakech, MPH, is a PhD Candidate in Health Policy and Equity at York University. His research interests include the social determinants of health, public policy, health equity and the political economy of health. He contributed the section on **Race**.

Ronald Labonté, PhD, is Distinguished Professor and former Canada Research Chair in Globalization and Health Equity in the School of Epidemiology and Public Health, University of Ottawa; and Professor, College of Medicine and Public Health, Flinders University, Australia. He contributed the section on **Globalization**.

Ambreen Sayani, MD, PhD, Health Policy and Equity, holds a Canadian Institutes of Health Research funded Postdoctoral Fellowship in Patient-Oriented research at Women's College Hospital, Toronto and is a Research Affiliate at the MAP-Centre for Urban Health Solutions, St. Michael's Hospital. She contributed the section on **Immigration**.

Printed and bound colour copies of this document are available.

Details are provided at www.thecanadianfacts.org

FOREWORD TO THE SECOND EDITION

The World Health Organization's Commission on Social Determinants of Health's final report in 2008 entitled *Closing the Gap in a Generation: Health Equity through Action on the Social Determinants of Health* demonstrated how the conditions in which people live and work directly affect their health. Health inequities are differences in health that result from the social conditions in which people live, are systematic across a population, and are considered unfair since most can be avoided. Health inequities are a serious and growing public health issue locally, nationally, and globally. A key approach to reducing health inequities is to address these issues by investing in the social determinants of health that contribute to the majority of health inequities. Creating opportunities for all people to be healthy and lead a dignified life is more than a health issue, it is also a matter of social justice.

It is a real pleasure to write the foreword to the *Social Determinants of Health: The Canadian Facts, 2nd edition.* The first edition, downloaded close to one million times over the past 10 years, provided an accessible and concise introduction to the social determinants of health and contributed significantly to shifting our thinking about what contributes to health and health inequities and what we can do to promote health and reduce these health equities. In this 2nd edition, authors Dennis Raphael, Toba Bryant, Juha Mikkonen and Alexander Raphael provide a very welcome updated perspective on each of the 17 social determinants of health as well as further details of how they matter even more today. This second edition of *The Canadian Facts* is well-organized, easy to use, and provides a comprehensive source of Canadian data and information about these 17 key social determinants of health which so strongly shape the health of Canadians. This document will be widely used by students, researchers, academics, practitioners, civil society, professional and community organizations, as well as policy and decision makers.

As one of six National Collaborating Centres funded by the Public Health Agency of Canada to 2028, the National Collaborating Centre for Determinants of Health (NCCDH) translates and exchanges knowledge and evidence to address the social determinants of health and promote health equity. We support knowledge use to improve health systems, specifically public health systems, including practice, programs, services, structures, research and policies. *The Social Determinants of Health: The Canadian Facts* is a 'go to' resource for the NCCDH and its partners.

As the honorable Monique Bégin said in the foreword to the 1st edition, the *"Social Determinants of Health: The Canadian Facts,* is about us, Canadian society, and what we need to put faces and voices to the inequities – and the health inequities in particular – that exist in our midst."* She predicted that providing a concrete description of the complex and challenging problems that exist across Canada in terms of the social determinants of health would move us to action. This 2nd edition provides an updated description of these "facts" and is certain to be an impetus for real action at all levels.

Claire Betker, RN, PhD, CCHN(C)
Scientific Director | Directrice scientifique

National Collaborating Centre for Determinants of Health | Centre de collaboration nationale des déterminants de la santé

St. Francis Xavier University | Université St. Francis Xavier

FOREWORD TO THE FIRST EDITION

We have known for a very long time that health inequities exist. These inequities affect all Canadians but they have especially strong impacts upon the health of those living in poverty. Adding social sciences evidence – the understanding of social structures and of power relationships – we have now accumulated indisputable evidence that *social injustice is killing people on a grand scale.*

When the World Health Organization's Commission on Social Determinants of Health published its final report (containing the quote above) that demonstrated how the conditions in which people live and work directly affect the quality of their health, we nodded in agreement. Everyone agrees that populations of Bangladesh, Sierra Leone or Haiti have low life expectancy, are malnourished, live in fearful and unhealthy environments, and are having a terrible time just trying to survive.

But what does that have to do with us in Canada?

For years, we bragged that we were identified by the United Nations as "the best country in the world in which to live". We have since dropped a few ranks, but our bragging continues. We would be the most surprised to learn that, in all countries – and that includes Canada – health and illness follow a social gradient: the lower the socioeconomic position, the worse the health.

The truth is that Canada – the ninth richest country in the world – is so wealthy that it manages to mask the reality of poverty, social exclusion and discrimination, the erosion of employment quality, its adverse mental health outcomes, and youth suicides. While one of the world's biggest spenders in health care, we have one of the worst records in providing an effective social safety net. What good does it do to treat people's illnesses, to then send them back to the conditions that made them sick?

This wonderful document, *Social Determinants of Health: The Canadian Facts,* is about us, Canadian society, and what we need to put faces and voices to the inequities – and the health inequities in particular – that exist in our midst. Only when we see a concrete description of these complex and challenging problems, when we read about their various expressions in all the regions of the country and among the many sub-groups making up Canada, can we move to action.

A document like this one, accessible and presenting the spectrum of existing inequities in health, will promote awareness and informed debate, and I welcome its publication. Following years of a move towards the ideology of individualism, a growing number of Canadians are anxious to reconnect with the concept of a just society and the sense of solidarity it envisions. Health inequities are not a problem just of the poor. It is **our** challenge and it is about public policies and political choices and our commitments to making these happen.

I find it an honour to write this Foreword to *Social Determinants of Health: The Canadian Facts,* a great initiative of our Canadian advocate for population health, Dennis Raphael, and his colleague from Finland, Juha Mikkonen.

The Hon. Monique Bégin, PC, FRSC, OC

Member of WHO Commission on
Social Determinants of Health

Former Minister of
National Health & Welfare

WHAT PEOPLE ARE SAYING ABOUT THE CANADIAN FACTS

"Perhaps now more than ever, Canadians need a straightforward reminder of what is really important to health. The Canadian Facts reminds us that as we worry about the sustainability of the health care system, what we really need to focus on is how to keep people healthy in the first place. Investing in the underlying determinants of health and creating equal opportunities for all for health is fundamental to a prosperous and just society. Kudos to the authors for continuing to make readily accessible the up-to-date Canadian Facts underlying this critical message."
– Penny Sutcliffe, MD, MHSc, FRCPC, Medical Officer of Health/Chief
    Executive Officer, Public Health Sudbury & Districts

"Dennis Raphael, Toba Bryant, Juha Mikkonen and Alexander Raphael have created the go-to guide to social determinants of health in Canada. I consult it regularly, and consider it an essential tool for research, education, and advocacy. I regularly recommend it to clinicians, students, policymakers, journalists and health system designers. It has been a game-changer, providing us with a simple, reliable guide to defining and understanding the social determinants of health. This book should be the first off the shelf for anyone looking to reduce health inequities in Canada."
– Gary Bloch, Family Physician, St. Michael's Hospital, Toronto; Associate
    Professor, University of Toronto

"The Canadian Facts Second Edition is a pivotal document, succinctly demonstrating the evidence of Canadian public policy makers' staunch and persistent resistance to action on the social determinants of health. Canada is at a tipping point in terms of neoliberal public policy denial of the facts of worsening wealth inequality and the racialization and marginalization of poverty in our country. The Canadian Facts are the facts of social murder and structural violence laid bare for all of us, especially those with governance power, to wake up and take responsibility and action. The entire document is a call to action to decrease and halt injustices and name the beneficiaries of market-driven and morally bankrupt wealth accumulation in Canada—the hidden side of worsening inequality and its entirely avoidable consequences. The Canadian Facts demonstrates that other countries have successfully tackled wealth distribution for the collective and compassionate good of all. We can too."
– Elizabeth McGibbon, Professor, St. Francis Xavier University

WHAT PEOPLE ARE SAYING ABOUT THE CANADIAN FACTS

"Under the International Covenant on Economic, Social and Cultural Rights, everyone has rights 'to an adequate standard of living' and 'the enjoyment of the highest attainable standard of physical and mental health.' Nonetheless, the evidence for comprehensive action on the social determinants of health is overwhelming. Like highly skilled trial lawyers, the authors have assembled this evidence, concisely, clearly and compellingly, into a single document. As a result, the prospect of realizing the rights that constitute an international standard for a decent human life is that much brighter. Bravo!"
   – Rob Rainer, Former Executive Director, Canada Without Poverty

"The Canadian Facts so succinctly described in this readable little book are not nice ones. But beneath the intersecting pathways by which social injustices become health inequalities lies the most sobering message: Things are getting worse. We have lived through three decades where the predatory greed of unregulated markets has allowed (and still allows) some to accumulate ever larger hordes of wealth and power while denying others a fair share of the resources they need to be healthy. This book is a fast-fact reference and an invitation for Canadian health workers to join with social movement activists elsewhere to reclaim for the public good some of these appropriated resources. "
   – Ronald Labonté, Professor and Distinguished Research Chair in Globalization
      and Health Equity, University of Ottawa

"With unusual clarity and insight, this informative resource will help change the way readers think about health. It renders visible how underlying social and economic environments influence health outcomes even more than personal behaviors, genetic profiles, or access to healthcare. Solutions, it reminds us, lie not in new medical advances or even 'right choices,' but in the political arena: struggling for the social changes that can provide every resident the opportunity to live a healthy and fulfilling life."
   – Larry Adelman, creator and executive producer, Unnatural Causes: Is
      Inequality Making Us Sick?

1. INTRODUCTION

A health care system – even the best health care system in the world – will be only one of the ingredients that determine whether your life will be long or short, healthy or sick, full of fulfillment, or empty with despair.

– The Honourable Roy Romanow, 2004

The primary factors that shape the health of Canadians are not medical treatments or lifestyle choices but rather the living and working conditions they experience. These conditions have come to be known as the social determinants of health (Figure 1.1). The importance to health of living conditions was established in the mid-1800s and has been enshrined in Canadian government policy documents since the mid-1970s. In fact, Canadian contributions to the social determinants of health concept have been so extensive as to make Canada a "health promotion powerhouse" in the eyes of the international health community. Reports from Canada's Chief Public Health Officer, the Public Health Agency of Canada, and Statistics Canada continue to document the importance of the social determinants of health.

But this information – based on decades of research and hundreds of studies in Canada and elsewhere – tells a story unfamiliar to many Canadians. Canadians are only now becoming more aware that our health is shaped by how income and wealth is distributed, whether we are employed, and if so, the working conditions we experience. Furthermore, our well-being is also determined by the health and social services we receive and our ability to obtain quality education, food and housing, among other factors. And contrary to the assumption that Canadians have personal control over these factors, in most cases these living and working conditions are – for better or worse – imposed upon us by the quality of the communities, housing situations, our work settings, health and social service agencies, and educational institutions with which we interact. The COVID-19 crisis has dramatically placed these issues in front of Canadians as those who are already disadvantaged are not only more likely to contract and succumb to COVID-19 but are also the ones bearing the brunt of its adverse economic effects.

There is much evidence that the quality of the social determinants of health Canadians experience explain the wide health inequalities that exist among Canadians. How long Canadians live and whether they experience cardiovascular disease, adult-onset diabetes, respiratory disease and a host of other afflictions is very much determined by their living and working conditions. The same goes for the health of their children: differences among Canadian children in their surviving beyond their first year of life, experiencing childhood afflictions such as asthma and injuries, and whether they fall behind in school are strongly related to the social determinants of health they experience.

Research is also finding that the quality of these health-shaping living conditions is powerfully determined by decisions governments make in a range of different public policy domains.

Governments at the municipal, provincial/territorial, and federal levels create policies, laws, and regulations that influence how much income Canadians receive through employment, family benefits, or social assistance, the quality and availability of affordable housing, the kinds of health and social services and recreational opportunities they can access, and what happens when Canadians lose their jobs during economic downturns.

These experiences also provide the best explanations for how Canada compares to other nations in overall health. Canadians generally enjoy better health than Americans, but do not do as well when compared to many other nations with public policies that strengthen the quality and provide more equitable distribution of the social determinants of health. Indeed, the World Health Organization sees health damaging experiences as resulting from "a toxic combination of poor social policies and programmes, unfair economic arrangements, and bad politics".

Despite this evidence, there is rather little effort by Canadian governments and policymakers to improve the quality and equitable distribution of the social determinants of health through public policy action. Canada compares unfavourably to other wealthy nations in its support of citizens as they navigate the life course. Our income inequality is increasing, and our poverty rates are amongst the highest of wealthy nations. Canadian spending in support of families, persons with disabilities, older Canadians, and employment training is among the lowest of these same wealthy nations.

Social Determinants of Health: The Canadian Facts, 2nd edition, provides Canadians with an updated introduction to the social determinants of our health. We first explain how living conditions "get under the skin" to either promote health or cause disease.

We then explain, for each of the 17 social determinants of health:

1)   Why it is important to health;
2)   How we compare on the social determinant of health to other wealthy developed nations; and
3)   How the quality of the specific social determinant can be improved.

Key sources are provided for each social determinant of health. We conclude with a section that outlines what Canadians can do to improve the quality and equitable distribution of the social determinants of health. An epilogue places these concepts within a welfare state analysis.

Social Determinants of Health: The Canadian Facts, 2nd edition is a companion to two other information sources about the social determinants of health. *Social Determinants of Health: Canadian Perspectives*, 3rd edition (2016) is an extensive compilation of prominent Canadian scholars and researchers' analyses of the state of the social determinants of health in Canada. *About Canada: Health and Illness*, 2nd edition (2016) provides this information in a more compact and accessible format for the general public.

Improving the health of Canadians is possible but requires Canadians think about health and its determinants in a more sophisticated manner than has been the case to date. The purpose of this second edition of *Social Determinants of Health: The Canadian Facts* is to stimulate research, advocacy, and public debate about the social determinants of health and means of improving their quality and making their distribution more equitable.

The Authors

Key sources

Bryant, T. (2016). Health Policy in Canada, 2nd edition. Toronto: Canadian Scholars' Press.

Bryant, T., & Raphael, D. (2020). The Politics of Health in the Canadian Welfare State. Toronto: Canadian Scholars' Press.

Raphael, D. (2016). About Canada: Health and Illness, 2nd edition. Halifax: Fernwood Publishers.

Raphael, D. (Ed.). (2016). Social Determinants of Health: Canadian Perspectives, 3rd edition. Toronto: Canadian Scholars' Press.

World Health Organization. (2008). Closing the Gap in a Generation: Health Equity through Action on the Social Determinants of Health. Geneva: WHO.

Figure 1.1 A Model of the Determinants of Health

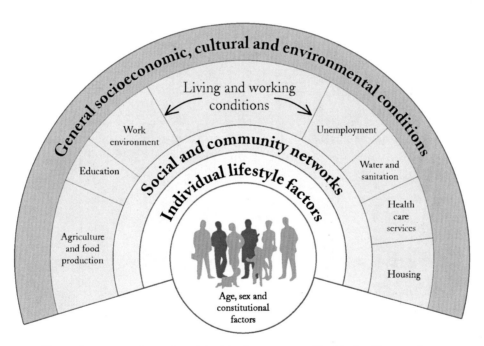

Figure shows one influential model of the determinants of health that illustrates how various health-influencing factors are embedded within broader aspects of society.

Source: Dahlgren, G. and Whitehead, M. (1991). Policies and Strategies to Promote Social Equity in Health. Stockholm: Institute for Futures Studies.

Figure 1.2 Social Determinants of Health

Among the variety of models of the social determinants of health that exist, the one developed at a York University Conference held in Toronto in 2002 has proven especially useful for understanding why some Canadians are healthier than others. The 17 social determinants of health in this model are:

disability
early child development
education
employment and working conditions
food insecurity
gender
geography
globalization
health services
housing
immigration
income and income distribution
Indigenous ancestry
race
social exclusion
social safety net
unemployment and job security

Each of these social determinants of health has been shown to have strong effects upon the health of Canadians. These effects are actually much stronger than the ones associated with behaviours such as diet, physical activity, and even tobacco and excessive alcohol use.

Source: Raphael, D. (Ed.) (2016). Social Determinants of Health: Canadian Perspectives, 3rd edition.
Toronto: Canadian Scholars' Press.

2. STRESS, BODIES, AND ILLNESS

Prolonged stress, or rather the responses it engenders, are known to have deleterious effects on a number of biological systems and to give rise to a number of illnesses.

– Robert Evans, 1994

Why Is It Important?

People who endure adverse living and working conditions experience concrete material and social deprivation that adversely affect health. These experiences also cause high levels of physiological and psychological stress. These stressful experiences arise from conditions of low income, poor quality housing, food insecurity, inadequate working conditions, insecure employment, and various forms of discrimination based on Indigenous ancestry, disability, gender, immigrant status, and race. Lack of supportive relationships, social isolation, and mistrust of others associated with material and social deprivation further increases stress.

At the physiological level, chronic stress leads to prolonged biological reactions that strain the physical body. Stressful situations and continuing threats provoke "fight-or-flight" reactions. These reactions impose chronic stress upon the body if a person does not have enough opportunities for recovery in non-stressful environments. Research evidence convincingly shows that continuous stress – or allostatic load – beginning during childhood weakens resistance to disease and disrupts the functioning of the hormonal, metabolic, and immune systems. Physiological processes provoked by stress make people more vulnerable to many serious illnesses such as cardiovascular disease, adult-onset diabetes, respiratory, and autoimmune diseases, among others.

At the psychological level, stressful and poor living conditions cause continuing feelings of shame, insecurity and worthlessness. Under adverse living conditions, everyday life often appears as unpredictable, uncontrollable, and meaningless. Uncertainty about the future raises anxiety and hopelessness that creates exhaustion and makes everyday coping difficult. People who experience high levels of stress often attempt to relieve these pressures by adopting unhealthy coping behaviours, such as excessive use of alcohol, tobacco use, and overeating. These behaviours are generally known to be unhealthy in the long term but are effective in bringing temporary relief. Damaging behaviours, therefore, should be seen as coping responses to adverse life circumstances even though they make the situation worse in the long run. These life circumstances are fundamental causes of disease whose effects operate through various pathways to causes disease.

Stressful living conditions make it extremely hard to take up physical leisure activity or practice healthy eating habits because most of one's energy is directed towards coping with day-to-day life. Similarly, taking drugs – either prescribed or illegal – relieves the symptoms of stress. Healthy living programs aimed at those at risk are not very effective in improving health and quality of life. This is because in many cases, individually oriented physical activity and healthy eating programs do not address the social determinants of health that are the underlying causes of most illnesses. Such programs may actually increase health inequities because they are most likely to be taken up by those already at low risk of adverse health outcomes.

Figure 2.1 Social Determinants of Health and the Pathways to Health and Illness

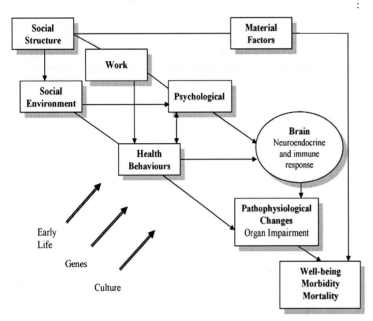

Source: Brunner, E., & Marmot, M. G. (2006). 'Social Organization, Stress, and Health.' In M. G. Marmot & R. G. Wilkinson (Eds.), Social Determinants of Health. Oxford: Oxford University Press, Figure 2.2, p. 9.

Figure 2.1 shows how the organization of society influences the living and working conditions we experience that then go on to shape health. These processes operate through material, psychosocial, and behavioural pathways. At all stages of life, genetics, early life, and cultural factors are also strong influences upon health.

Policy Implications

• Promoting health and reducing illness requires a focus on the sources of problems rather than dealing with symptoms. Therefore, the most effective way to improve health is by improving the living and working conditions people experience, thereby reducing the material and social deprivation and physiological and psychological stress that leads to illness.

• Elected representatives and decision-makers must commit themselves to implementing public policy that ensures high quality and more equitable distribution of the social determinants of health for every Canadian. This means dealing with the fundamental causes of adverse health outcomes, the problematic living and working conditions that: a) directly threaten health; b) create stress that wears out bodies; and c) causes the uptake of health threatening behaviours.

Key sources

Brunner, E. & Marmot, M. G. (2006). Social organization, stress, and health. In Marmot M. G. & Wilkinson, R. G. (Eds.) (2006). Social Determinants of Health, 2nd edition (pp. 6-30). Oxford, UK: Oxford University Press.

Danese, A. & McEwen, B.S. (2012). Adverse childhood experiences, allostasis, allostatic load, and age-related disease. Physiology & Behavior, 106, 29-39.

Link, B.G. & Phelan J. (1995) Social conditions as fundamental causes of disease. Journal of Health and Social Behavior, (extra issue), 80-94.

Raphael, D. (2016). Social structure, living conditions, and health. In Raphael, D. (Ed.), Social Determinants of Health: Canadian Perspectives, 3rd edition (pp. 32-58). Toronto: Canadian Scholars' Press.

3. INCOME AND INCOME DISTRIBUTION

Health researchers have demonstrated a clear link between income and socio-economic status and health outcomes, such that longevity and state of health rise with position on the income scales.

– Andrew Jackson and Govind Rao, 2016

Why Is It Important?

Income is perhaps the most important social determinant of health. Level of income shapes overall living conditions that affect physiological and psychological functioning and the take-up of health-related behaviours such as quality of diet, extent of physical activity, tobacco use, and excessive alcohol use. In Canada, income determines the quality of other social determinants of health such as food security, housing, education, early child development, and other prerequisites of health.

The relationship between income and health can be studied at two different levels. First, we can observe how health is related to the actual income that an individual or family receives. Second, we can study how income is distributed across the population and how this distribution is related to the overall health of the population. More equal income distribution has proven to be one of the best predictors of better overall health of a society. Income comes to be especially important in societies that provide fewer important services and benefits as a matter of right. In Canada, general government revenues fund public education until grade 12, necessary medically procedures, and libraries, but childcare, housing, post-secondary education, employment training, recreational opportunities, prescription drugs, dental care and resources for retirement must be bought and paid for by individuals. In contrast, in many wealthy nations these benefits and services are universally provided as citizen rights.

Low income leads to material and social deprivation. The greater the deprivation, the less likely individuals and families are able to afford the basic prerequisites of health such as food, clothing, and housing. Deprivation also contributes to social exclusion by making it harder to participate in cultural, educational, and recreational activities. In the long run, material and social deprivation and the social exclusion it engenders affects one's health and lessens the abilities to live fulfilling lives free of health problems. Having income so low as to constitute living in poverty is especially dangerous to health.

Researchers find that men in the wealthiest 20 percent of neighbourhoods in Canada live on average more than five years longer than men in the poorest 20 percent of neighbourhoods (Figure 3.1). The comparative difference for women is more than two years. Suicide rates in the lowest income neighbourhoods are almost twice those in the wealthiest neighbourhoods. Additionally, a host of studies show that heart disease, adult-onset diabetes, and respiratory disease are far more common among low-income Canadians. Infant mortality rates are 46 percent higher in the poorest 20 percent of neighbourhoods than in the richest 20 percent.

A Canadian study that followed individuals over time found men in the lowest 20 percent quintile of income have death rates 67 percent higher than the wealthiest 20 percent. For women, the figure is 52 percent. If the death rates for all Canadians were similar to those of the wealthiest 20 percent of Canadians, there would be 19 percent fewer deaths for men and 17 percent fewer for women every year. This is equal to 40,000 fewer deaths a year; 25,000 for men and 15,000 for women. Income differences in health outcomes are seen right across the income gradient from rich to poor.

Canada's overall level of income inequality is above the OECD average (Figure 3.2). As a result of these trends, from 1980 to 2015, the bottom 60 percent of Canadian families experienced very small increases in market incomes in constant dollars while the top 20 percent of Canadian families did very well. After taxes and government transfers, this picture improves somewhat with slight increases for the bottom 60 percent of Canadians, but these increases are dwarfed by the increases experienced by the wealthiest 20 percent of Canadians.

Increasing income inequality has led to a hollowing out of the middle class in Canada with significant increases from 1980-2015 in the percentages of Canadian families who are poor or very rich. The percentage of Canadian families who earned middle-level incomes declined from 1980 to 2015 while the percentage of very wealthy Canadians increased as did those near the bottom of the income distribution. There is good reason to think these trends are intensifying.

The increases in wealth inequality in Canada are even more troubling. Wealth is probably a better indicator of long-term health outcomes as it is a better measure of financial security than income. In 2019, the bottom 20 percent of Canadians were on average in debt for $500 while the average net worth of the wealthiest 20 percent of Canadians was $2,480,300. Indeed, almost half of Canadian families (47 percent) say they would be in financial difficulty if their paycheck was a week late. Thirty-five per cent said they feel overwhelmed by their level of debt. Since this was the situation before the economic upheavals of the COVID-19 crisis, the situation for many Canadians is now much worse.

Policy Implications

• There is an emerging consensus that income inequality is a key health policy issue that needs to be addressed by governments and policymakers.

• Increasing the minimum wage to a living wage and boosting social assistance levels for those unable to work would provide immediate health benefits for the most disadvantaged Canadians.

• Reducing inequalities in income and wealth through progressive taxation and using these revenues to provide universal programs and services are among the best ways of improving health in a society.

• More unionized workplaces would reduce income and wealth inequalities in Canada, thereby improving health. Unionization helps to set limits on extreme profit-making that comes at the expense of employees' health and wellbeing.

Key sources

Auger, N., & Alix, C. (2016). Income, income distribution, and health in Canada. In D. Raphael (Ed.), Social Determinants of Health: Canadian Perspectives, 3rd edition (pp. 90-109). Toronto: Canadian Scholars' Press.

Canadian Press (2017). Almost half of Canadian employees living paycheque to paycheque, survey indicates. Ottawa: Author. Available at https://www.cbc.ca/news/business/payroll-salary-survey-1.4276782

Curry-Stevens, A. (2016). Precarious changes: A generational exploration. In D. Raphael (Ed.), Social Determinants of Health: Canadian Perspectives, 3rd edition (pp. 60-89). Toronto: Canadian Scholars' Press.

Public Health Agency of Canada and Pan-Canadian Public Health Network. (2018). Key Health Inequalities in Canada: A National Portrait. Ottawa: Author.

Statistics Canada (2021). Assets and Debts by Net Worth Quintile, Canada, Provinces and Selected Census Metropolitan Areas, Survey of Financial Security. Ottawa: Author. Available at https://www150.statcan.gc.ca/t1/tbl1/en/tv.action?pid=111 0004901&pickMembers%5B0%5D=1.1&pickMembers%5B1%5D=2.27&pickMembers%5B2%5D=4.6&cubeTimeFrame. startYear=2005&cubeTimeFrame.endYear=2019&referencePeriods=20050101%2C20190101

Tjepkema, M., Wilkins, R., & Long, A. (2013). Cause-specific mortality by income adequacy in Canada: A 16-year follow-up study. Health Reports, 24(7), 14-22.

Figure 3.1 Life Expectancy of Females and Males by Income Quintile of Neighbourhood, Canada, 2009-2011

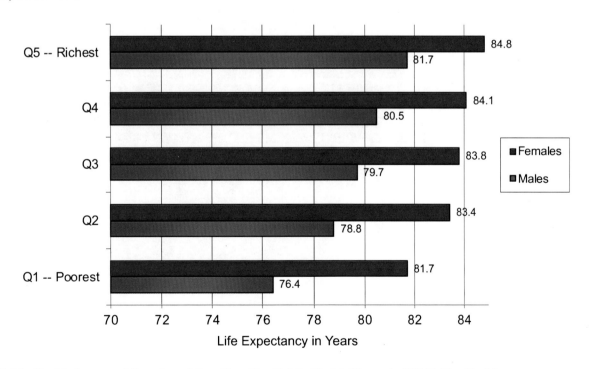

Source: Public Health Agency of Canada and Pan-Canadian Public Health Network. (2018). Key Health Inequalities in Canada: A National Portrait. Ottawa: Author.

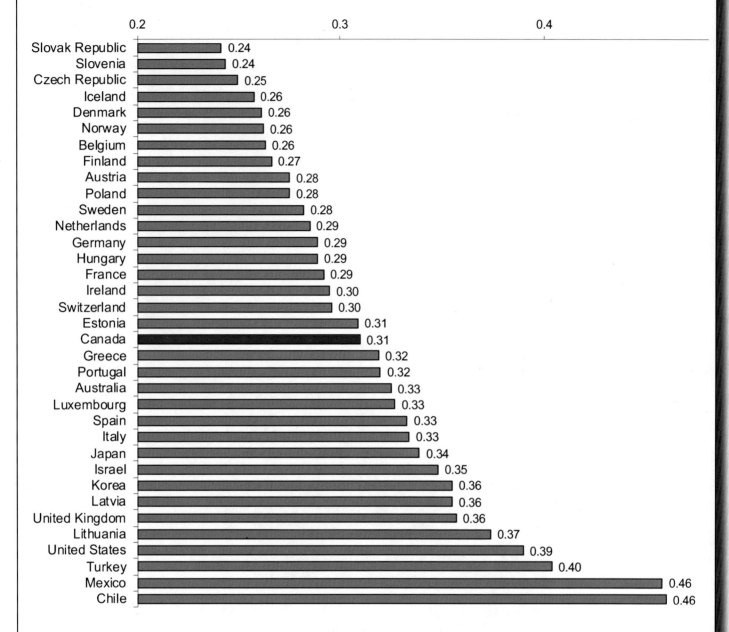

Figure 3.2 Income Inequality in OECD Nations, 2019

Country	Gini Coefficient
Slovak Republic	0.24
Slovenia	0.24
Czech Republic	0.25
Iceland	0.26
Denmark	0.26
Norway	0.26
Belgium	0.26
Finland	0.27
Austria	0.28
Poland	0.28
Sweden	0.28
Netherlands	0.29
Germany	0.29
Hungary	0.29
France	0.29
Ireland	0.30
Switzerland	0.30
Estonia	0.31
Canada	0.31
Greece	0.32
Portugal	0.32
Australia	0.33
Luxembourg	0.33
Spain	0.33
Italy	0.33
Japan	0.34
Israel	0.35
Korea	0.36
Latvia	0.36
United Kingdom	0.36
Lithuania	0.37
United States	0.39
Turkey	0.40
Mexico	0.46
Chile	0.46

Gini Coefficient of Income Inequality

Note: Countries are ranked in increasing order in the Gini coefficient. The income concept used is that of disposable household income in cash, adjusted for household size.

Source: Organization for Economic Co-operation and Development (2020). Income inequality. Available at https://data.oecd.org/inequality/income-inequality.htm

4. EDUCATION

Canada as a whole performs well on national and international assessments, but disparities exist among populations and regions that do not seem to be diminishing with time.

– Charles Ungerleider and Tracey Burns, 2016

Why Is It Important?

Education is an important social determinant of health. People with higher education tend to be healthier than those with lower educational attainment. There are various pathways by which education leads to better health. First, level of education is highly correlated with other social determinants of health such as the level of income, employment security, and working conditions. Viewed in this light, education helps people to move up the socioeconomic ladder and provides better access to economic and social resources.

Second, higher education makes it easier to enact larger overall changes in the Canadian employment market. Better educated citizens have more opportunities to benefit from new training opportunities if their employment situation suddenly changes. Furthermore, education facilitates citizens' possibilities for civic activities and engagement in the political process. In other words, people attain better understanding of the world and they become more able to see and influence societal factors that shape their own health.

Finally, education increases overall literacy and understanding of how one can promote one's own health through individual action. With higher education, people attain more sophisticated skills to evaluate how behaviours they adopt might be harmful or beneficial to their health. They achieve

greater ability and more resources to allow attainment of healthier lifestyles.

On the other hand, it is important to remember that lack of education in itself is not the main factor causing poorer health. The manner by which education influences the population's health is shaped by public policies. For instance, if adequate income and necessary services such as childcare and job training are available to all, the health-threatening effects of having less education would be much less. In addition, the link between parents' educational levels and their children's achievement are weaker when the social determinants of health are more equitably distributed, allowing for greater intergenerational mobility.

In international comparisons, the overall state of education in Canada is good (Figure 4.1). Canada is one of a few wealthy nations where immigrant children and children of immigrants perform as well as children born in Canada to Canadian-born parents. Fifty three percent of the population have post-secondary education. However, the troubling aspect in Canada is that children whose parents do not have post-secondary education perform notably worse than children of more educated parents. It has been suggested that the link between children's educational performance with parents' education levels would be reduced if there were affordable and high-quality early learning programs in Canada. The lack of these programs has a major influence on many children's intellectual and emotional development.

High tuition fees influence whether children of low-income families can attain college or university education. In Scandinavian countries that provide free post-secondary education, the link between family background and educational attainment is weaker than is the case in Canada. For example, Swedish children whose parents did not complete secondary school usually outperform children on language and mathematical skills from other nations – including Canada – whose parents completed post-secondary education.

Policy Implications

•   Elected representatives must commit themselves to adequately funding the Canadian education system so that schools are able to provide well-developed curricula for students.

•   Universal high-quality childcare would reduce the link between parents' and children's educational achievement levels, thereby promoting health.

•   Tuition fees for university and college education must be better managed, reduced or eliminated, so that fees do not exclude children of lower-income families from higher education.

Key sources

Frenette, M. (2017). Postsecondary Enrolment by Parental Income: Recent National and Provincial Trends. Ottawa: Statistics Canada. Available at https://www150.statcan.gc.ca/n1/pub/11-626-x/11-626-x2017070-eng.htm

OECD/EU (2018). Settling In 2018: Indicators of Immigrant Integration. Brussels: Author. Available at https://www.oecd.org/publications/indicators-of-immigrant-integration-2018-9789264307216-en.htm

Raphael, D. (2016). Key immigration issues in developed nations. In D. Raphael (Ed.), Immigration, Public Policy, and Health: Newcomer Experiences in Developed Nations (pp. 317-334). Toronto: Canadian Scholars' Press.

Ronson, B. & Rootman, I. (2016). Literacy and health literacy: New understandings about their impact on health. In D. Raphael (Ed.), Social Determinants of Health: Canadian Perspectives, 3rd edition (pp. 261-290). Toronto: Canadian Scholars' Press.

Ungerleider, C. & Burns, T. (2016). The state and quality of Canadian public elementary and secondary education. In D. Raphael (Ed.), Social Determinants of Health: Canadian Perspectives, 3rd edition (pp. 240-260). Toronto: Canadian Scholars' Press.

Figure 4.1 Mean PISA Reading Scores of 15 Year Olds with Different Migration Backgrounds, OECD Nations, 2015

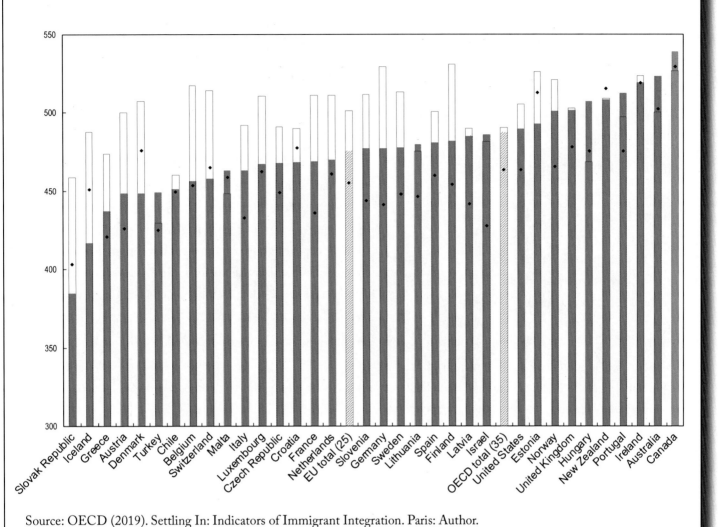

Source: OECD (2019). Settling In: Indicators of Immigrant Integration. Paris: Author.

5. UNEMPLOYMENT AND JOB SECURITY

Workers are not only more uncertain about the likelihood that they will be retained in their current job, they are also uncertain about whether they will be able to find another job that meets their needs.

– Emile Tompa, Michael Polanyi, and Janice Foley, 2016

Why Is It Important?

Employment provides income, a sense of identity, and helps to structure day-to-day life. Unemployment frequently leads to material and social deprivation, psychological stress, and the adoption of health-threatening coping behaviours. Unemployment is associated with physical and mental health problems that include depression, anxiety and increased suicide rates. Job insecurity causes exhaustion (burnout), general mental/psychological problems, poor self-rated health, and a variety of somatic complaints.

Job insecurity has been increasing in Canada during the past decades (Figure 5.1). Currently, less than two-thirds of Canadians have a regular or permanent full-time job. Only half of working aged Canadians have had a single full-time job for over six months or more. Precarious forms of work include arrangements such as working part-time (20.3 percent of Canadians), being self-employed (15.3 percent), or having temporary work (11.3 percent). The OECD calculates an employment protection index of rules and regulations that protects employment and provides benefits to temporary workers. Canada performs very poorly on this index, achieving a score that was ranked 35th of 36 nations (Figure 5.2).

Part-time work is reflecting greater income and employment insecurity: the percentage of men with part-time work as a main job is increasing while the percentage of women with part-time work as a main job is declining. Researchers suggest that these trends are associated with more intense work life, decreased job security and income polarization between the rich and poor.

Unemployment is related to poor health through various pathways. First, unemployment often leads to material deprivation and poverty by reducing income and removing benefits previously provided by one's employer. Second, losing a job is a stressful event that lowers one's self-esteem, disrupts daily routines, and increases anxiety. Third, unemployment increases the likelihood of turning to unhealthy coping behaviours such as tobacco use and problem drinking.

Often, insecure employment consists of intense work with non-standard working hours. Intense working conditions are associated with higher rates of stress, bodily pains, and a high risk of injury. Excessive hours of work increase chances of physiological and psychological problems such as sleep deprivation, high blood pressure, and heart disease. Consequently, job insecurity has negative effects on personal relationships, parenting effectiveness, and children's behaviour.

Women are over-represented in precarious forms of work. In 2018, 14 percent of employed women were temporary employees while the figure for men was 12.8 percent. Six percent of women were employed in involuntary part-time employment, while for men it was 3.8 percent. The OECD finds that Canada is ranked 12th highest amongst 32 nations in the proportion of total employment that is temporary. Finally, women, youth, seniors, and workers without post-secondary education are more likely to be working part-time or temporary jobs.

Policy Implications

•   National and international institutions need to be legally mandated to make agreements that provide the basic standards of employment and work for everyone.

•   Power inequalities between employers and employees need to be reduced through stronger legislation governing equal opportunity in hiring, pay, training, and career advancement.

•   Unemployed Canadians must be provided access to adequate income, training, and employment opportunities through enhanced government support.

•   Workers, employers, government officials, and researchers need to develop a new vision of what constitutes healthy and productive work.

•   More policy-relevant research must be pursued to support government's decision-making and provide an accurate and up-to-date picture of job security in Canada.

Key sources

De Witte H, Pienaar J and De Cuyper N. (2016). Review of 30 years of longitudinal studies on the association between job insecurity and health and well-being: Is there causal evidence? Australian Psychologist, 51, 18-31.

Fong, F. (2018). Navigating Precarious Employment in Canada: Who is Really at Risk? Toronto: Chartered Professional Accountants of Canada. Available at https://tinyurl.com/y7xpecel

Standing Committee on Human Resources, Skills and Social Development and the Status of Persons with Disabilities (2019). Precarious Work: Understanding the Changing Nature of Work in Canada. Ottawa: Author. Available at https://www.ourcommons.ca/Content/Committee/421/HUMA/Reports/RP10553151/humarp19/humarp19-e.pdf

Tompa, E., Polanyi, M. & Foley, J. (2016). Health consequences of labour market flexibility and worker insecurity. In D. Raphael (Ed.), Social Determinants of Health: Canadian Perspectives, 3rd edition (pp. 88-98). Toronto: Canadian Scholars' Press.

Tremblay, D. G. (2016). Precarious work and the labour market. In D. Raphael (Ed.), Social Determinants of Health: Canadian Perspectives, 3rd edition (pp. 110-129). Toronto: Canadian Scholars' Press.

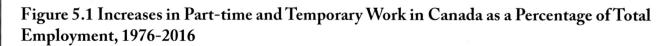

Figure 5.1 Increases in Part-time and Temporary Work in Canada as a Percentage of Total Employment, 1976-2016

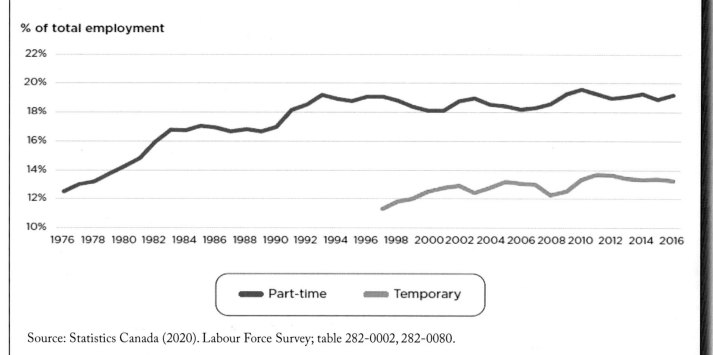

Source: Statistics Canada (2020). Labour Force Survey; table 282-0002, 282-0080.

Figure 5.2 Employment Protection, OECD Nations, 2019

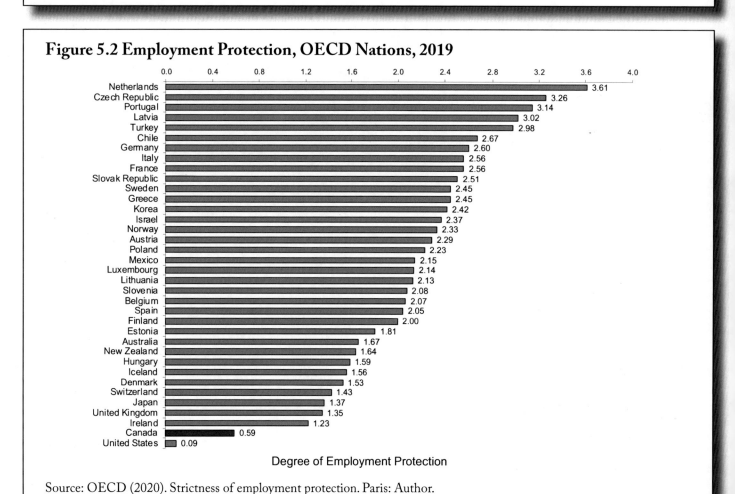

Degree of Employment Protection

Source: OECD (2020). Strictness of employment protection. Paris: Author.
Available at https://stats.oecd.org/Index.aspx?DataSetCode=EPL_OV#

6. EMPLOYMENT AND WORKING CONDITIONS

The relationship between working conditions and health outcomes is an important public health concern.

– Peter Smith and Michael Polanyi, 2016

Why Is It Important?

Working conditions are an important social determinant of health because of the great amount of time we spend in our workplaces. People who are already most vulnerable to poor health outcomes due to their lower income and education are also the ones most likely to experience health threatening working conditions.

Researchers have identified a host of work dimensions which shape health outcomes. The dimensions include factors such as: 1) employment security; 2) physical conditions at work; 3) work pace and stress; 4) working hours; and 5) opportunities for self-expression and individual development at work. Research evidence has also shown that imbalances between efforts to meet demands (e.g., time pressures, responsibility) and rewards (e.g., salary, respect from supervisors) often lead to significant health problems. When workers perceive that their efforts are not being adequately rewarded, they are more likely to develop a range of physical and mental afflictions (Figure 6.1).

Similarly, increased health problems are seen among workers who experience high demands but have little control over how to meet these demands. These high-stress jobs predispose individuals to high blood pressure, cardiovascular diseases, and development of physical and psychological difficulties such as depression and anxiety. High-strain jobs are especially common among low-income women working in the sales and service sector. Canadian women score higher than men in reporting high stress levels from "too many hours or too many demands."

A 2016 Statistics Canada survey reported that 10.5 percent of Canadians felt they might lose their job in the next six months. Forty-eight percent did not feel their job "offers good prospects for career advancement." The same survey found 26.2 percent felt that the workload was "not manageable", and 25.2 percent "often could not complete their assigned work during regular hours." Finally, 33.6 percent could not "choose their sequence of tasks" and 23 percent could not "provide input into work decisions."

Statistics Canada found in a 2010 study a rather large prevalence of work-related stress among Canadians. Almost 5.5 percent reported work was extremely stressful, 23.3 percent reported it was quite a bit stressful, and 41.5 percent reported it as a bit stressful. Canadians whose jobs were extremely stressful were three times more likely than non-stressed Canadians to have been treated for a mental health problem the past year. Those with jobs being a bit stressful had twice the risk of having been treated for this problem.

About 30 percent of Canadians had jobs with positives scores on most of six job dimensions of prospects, work intensity, working-time quality, skills and discretion, social environment, and income and benefits, while 26 percent had jobs with poor quality job scores in most of these dimensions. Not surprisingly, these poor-quality jobs were likely to be non-standard or precarious. About one-third to one-half of these workers were in the poorest job quality class.

According to data collected by the Association of Workers' Compensation Boards of Canada, 902 workplace fatalities were recorded in Canada in 2013, down from 1,014 in 2010. As Canadians work on average 230 days per year, this means that there were nearly four work-related deaths per working day. Men are much more likely than women to die on the job. In 2011, the incidence of workplace death was 20 times higher among men than women: 8.6 deaths per 100,000 workers versus 0.4 deaths.

In Canada, working hours are becoming more polarized with increases in shorter and longer hours. About 19.3 percent of Canadians worked more than 40 hours a week overtime in 2019 and on average these Canadians worked 48 hours a week. In contrast, full-time workers in the European Union generally work less than 40 hours per week and some countries such as France, the Netherlands, and Germany are now close to a 35-hour per week norm. Holidays and vacation time are much greater in European nations than in Canada (Figure 6.2).

Collective bargaining helps to equalize the power balance between employers and employees. Union members working under a collective agreement receive higher wages, more benefits, and greater opportunities to influence their working conditions. Overall, union members earn almost 23 percent higher wages than non-union workers. For men,

the advantage is 12.5 percent, for women, 36.3 percent. For female childcare workers the union advantage is 63.7 percent. The union advantage is especially great for blue-collar and lower wage private services; these are the Canadians at greater risk of living in poverty. Only 32 percent of Canadians belong to labour unions and work under a collective agreement, a figure much lower than many other wealthy nations.

Policy Implications

• Government policies must support Canadians' working life so that demands upon workers and their rewards are balanced.

• Special focus should be on improving conditions of employees in high-strain jobs by improving personal control and moderating work demands and for those in low income jobs by providing adequate rewards for work effort.

• Collective and organized action through unionization of workplaces is an important means of balancing power between employers and employees, thereby improving working conditions and promoting health.

Figure 6.1 Key Dimensions of the Workplace Environment Related to Health

Work Dimension	*Description*
Job strain	Job strain exists when people's autonomy over their work and their ability to use their skills are low, while the psychological demands placed upon them are high.
Effort-reward imbalance	The "effort–reward imbalance" model underlines the health importance of rewards (monetary, esteem, respect from supervisors and colleagues) being in line with the demands (time pressures, interruptions, responsibility, pressure to work overtime). When efforts are perceived to be higher than rewards, this leads to emotional distress.
Organizational justice	Organizational justice reflects the extent to which people believe that their supervisor considers their viewpoints, shares information concerning decision making and treats individuals fairly.
Work hours	Work hours are the number of hours usually worked. It is likely that too many and too few hours are both related to health problems.
Status inconsistency	Status inconsistency refers to a situation where an individual's level of education is higher than the skills he or she requires for the occupation. This situation has also been termed "goal-striving stress."
Precarious work	Precarious employment describes work experiences that are associated with instability, lack of protection, insecurity across various dimensions of work, and social and economic vulnerability.

Source: Adapted from Smith, P. & Polanyi, M. (2016). Understanding and improving the world of work. In D. Raphael (Ed.), Social Determinants of Health: Canadian Perspectives, 3rd edition (pp. 171-188), Table 8.1, p.175. Toronto: Canadian Scholars' Press.

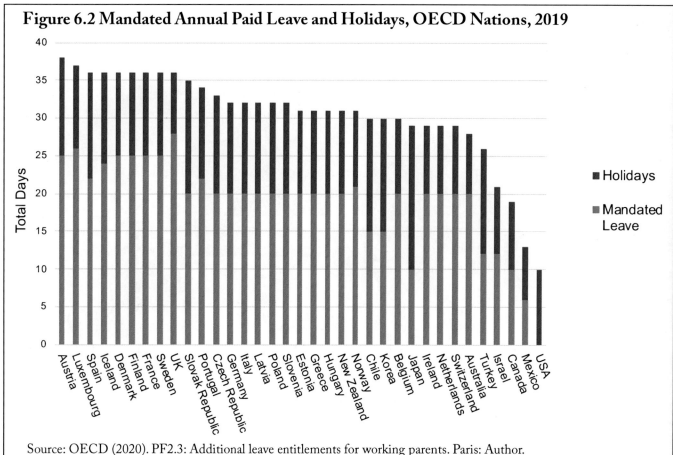

Figure 6.2 Mandated Annual Paid Leave and Holidays, OECD Nations, 2019

Source: OECD (2020). PF2.3: Additional leave entitlements for working parents. Paris: Author.
Available at https://www.oecd.org/els/soc/PF2_3_Additional_leave_entitlements_of_working_parents.pdf

Key sources

Chen, W. and Mehdi, T. (2018). Assessing Job Quality in Canada: A Multidimensional Approach. Ottawa: Statistics Canada. Available at https://www150.statcan.gc.ca/n1/pub/11f0019m/11f0019m2018412-eng.htm

Crompton, S. (2011). What's Stressing the Stressed? Main Sources of Stress among Workers. Ottawa: Statistics Canada. Available at https://www150.statcan.gc.ca/n1/en/pub/11-008-x/2011002/article/11562-eng.pdf?st=H2o-OYa3

Jackson, A. and Thomas, M. (2017). Work and Labour in Canada: Critical Issues, 3rd edition. Toronto: Canadian Scholars' Press.

Smith, P. & Polanyi, M. (2016). Understanding and improving the world of work. In D. Raphael (Ed.), Social Determinants of Health: Canadian Perspectives, 3rd edition (pp. 171-188). Toronto: Canadian Scholars' Press.

Statistics Canada (2020). Employees working overtime (weekly) by occupation, annual. Ottawa: Author. Available at https://www150.statcan.gc.ca/t1/tbl1/en/tv.action?pid=1410030901.

Szeto, A. C., & Dobson, K. S. (2013). Mental disorders and their association with perceived work stress: An investigation of the 2010 Canadian community health survey. Journal of Occupational Health Psychology, 18(2), 191-197.

7. EARLY CHILD DEVELOPMENT

There is strong evidence that early childhood experiences influence coping skills, resistance to health problems and overall health and well-being for the rest of one's life.

– Federal/Provincial/Territorial Advisory Committee on Population Health, 1996

Why Is It Important?

Early childhood experiences have strong immediate and longer lasting biological, psychological and social effects upon health.

"Latency effects" refer to how early childhood experiences predispose children to either good or poor health regardless of later life circumstances. For example, low birthweight babies living in disadvantaged conditions are generally more susceptible to health problems than babies of advantaged populations. These latency effects result from biological processes during pregnancy associated with poor maternal diet, parental risk behaviours, and experience of stress. Health effects may also result from early psychological experiences that create a sense of control or self-efficacy.

"Pathway effects" refer to a situation when children's exposures to risk factors at one point do not have immediate health effects but later lead to situations that do have health consequences. For instance, it is not an immediate health issue if young children lack readiness to learn as they enter school. But limited learning abilities can lead to experiences that are harmful to one's health in later life such as lower educational attainment which precludes well paid employment.

One way to weaken the relationship between parents' socioeconomic status and children's developmental outcomes is the provision of high-quality early child education regardless of parents' wealth.

"Cumulative effects" indicate that the longer children live under conditions of material and social deprivation, the more likely they are to show adverse developmental and health outcomes. Accumulated disadvantage can lead to cognitive and emotional deficits that make coping difficult. In addition, adverse childhood experiences can create a sense of inefficacy – or learned helplessness – which is a strong determinant of poor health.

The state of early child development in Canada is, however, cause for concern. A study by the Canadian Institute of Health Information found that 33 percent of boys and 19 percent of girls were vulnerable in at least one of the areas of physical health, social competence, emotional maturity, language and cognitive development, and communication skills and general knowledge.

The most obvious cause of this situation is whether children are living under conditions of material and social deprivation. The measure used by international organizations such as the OECD and the Innocenti Research Centre of the United

Nations International Children Emergency Fund defines child poverty as living in families which have access to less than 50 percent of the median family income of that nation. The OECD child poverty figure for Canada of 11.6 uses this metric. This figure gives Canada a rank of 18th of 36 wealthy developed nations (Figure 7.1).

In regard to access to regulated childcare – an important contributor to child well-being – only 20.5 percent of Canadian families have access to regulated child care. Even in Quebec where an extensive effort is underway to provide regulated high-quality childcare, only 37.4 percent of families have access to it. The Organisation for Economic Co-operation and Development published a report that rates Canada as last among 25 wealthy developed nations in meeting various early child development objectives. Canada is also one of the lowest spenders on supporting families with financial support for families and children. It allocates 1.6 percent of GDP, well below the OECD average of 2.0 percent, providing a rank of 25th of 36 nations (Figure 7.2). A comprehensive UNICEF report ranked Canada 25th of 41 wealthy nations in children's health and well-being using a wide range of health and social indicators.

The quality of early child development is shaped by the economic and social resources available to parents primarily through employment. Government can also provide a range of supports and benefits to children through family-friendly public policies. Researchers have even stated that establishing a comprehensive early childhood education program in Canada would be the single best means of improving Canadian health outcomes.

Policy Implications

•   Governments must guarantee that affordable and quality child care is available for all families regardless of wealth or income level.

•   Providing support and benefits to families through public policies forms a base for healthy child development. Providing higher wages and social assistance benefits would reduce child poverty and be one of the best means to improve early child development.

•   All Canadians would benefit from improved early child development in terms of improved community quality of life, reduced social problems, and improved Canadian economic performance.

Key sources

Friendly, M. (2016). Early childhood education and care as a social determinant of health. In D. Raphael (Ed.), Social Determinants of Health: Canadian Perspectives, 3rd edition (pp. 218-239). Toronto: Canadian Scholars' Press.

Hertzman, C., & Boyce, T. (2010). How experience gets under the skin to create gradients in developmental health. Annual Review of Public Health, 31, 329-347.

Irwin, K. G., Siddiqui, A., & Hertzman, C. (2007). Early Child Development: A Powerful Equalizer. Geneva: World Health Organization. Available at https://www.who.int/social_determinants/resources/ecd_kn_report_07_2007.pdf

Raphael, D. (2016). Early childhood development and health. In D. Raphael (Ed.) Social Determinants of Health: Canadian Perspectives, 3rd edition (pp. 218-239). Toronto: Canadian Scholars' Press.

UNICEF (2017). Building the Future: Children and the Sustainable Development Goals in Rich Countries. Innocenti: Innocenti Research Centre.

Figure 7.1 Percentage of Children Living in Poverty, OECD Nations, 2018

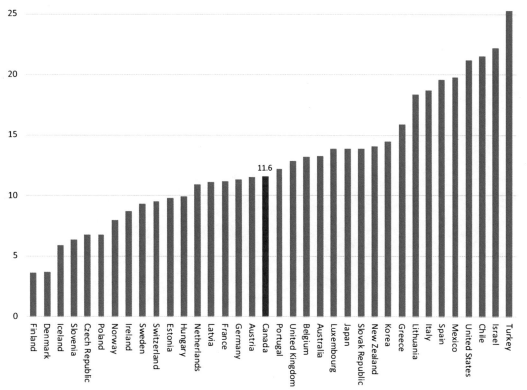

Source: Organisation for Economic Cooperation and Development. (2019). Poverty rate.
Available at: https://data.oecd.org/inequality/poverty-rate.htm

Figure 7.2 Public Expenditure on Family Benefits as % of GDP, OECD Nations, 2017

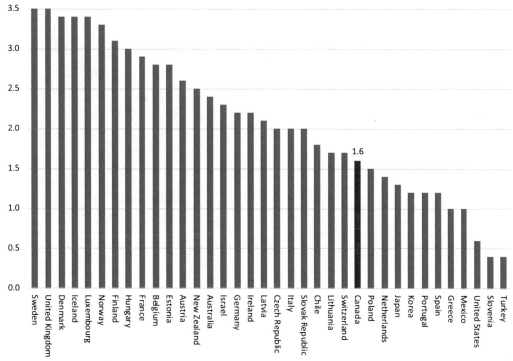

Source: Organisation for Economic Cooperation and Development (2020). Family benefits public spending. Available at
https://data.oecd.org/socialexp/family-benefits-public-spending.htm.

8. FOOD INSECURITY

A very brief social history of food insecurity in Canada would read simply: Poverty increased, then it deepened. Food insecurity emerged, then it increased in severity.

– Lynn McIntyre and Krista Rondeau, 2009

Why Is It Important?

Food is one of the basic human needs and is an important determinant of health and human dignity. Food insecure citizens are uncertain if they are able to acquire food in socially acceptable ways and is a barrier to adequate nutritional intake as they consume fewer servings of fruits and vegetables, milk products, and vitamins than those in food-secure households. Food insecure Canadians experience a variety of adverse health outcomes. The term *household food insecurity* (HFI) describes this situation.

Marginal HFI is worrying about running out of food and/or limited food selection due to a lack of money. Moderate HFI is consuming food inadequate in either quality or quantity, while severe HFI is experiencing reduced food intake or disrupted eating. The 2017-2018 Canadian Community Health Survey found that 12.7 per cent of Canadian households experienced some form of HFI.

Of this amount, 4.0 per cent experienced marginal HFI (approx. 552,000 households), 5.7 per cent experienced moderate HFI (approx. 819,000 households), and 3.0 per cent experienced severe HFI (approx. 429,900 households). Food insecurity is seen right across Canada (Figure 8.1).

Figures for families with children are higher at

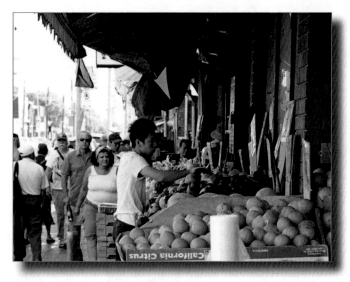

17.3 percent with rates for marginal HFI at 5.1 percent; moderate HFI at 8.3 percent; and 2.9 percent for severe HFI. HFI is at even more alarming levels among Canada's Indigenous populations. Provinces and territories with higher concentrations of First Nations and Inuit populations report higher rates of HFI (Nunavut, 57.0 percent; Northwest Territories, 21.6 percent; and Yukon, 16.9 percent). The risk of food insecurity is especially great in female lone-parent families (33.1 percent) and families receiving social assistance (60.4 percent).

A study identified many events that move a Canadian family into experiencing hunger. Hunger was found to result from a family acquiring another mouth to feed either through birth or family melding; a change in the number of parents in the home; loss of a job; change in employment hours; or decline in the health of an adult or a child. Getting out of hunger only happened under one condition: the mother began a full-time job, with the family's income rising.

Dietary deficiencies – more common among food insecure households – are associated with increased likelihood of chronic disease and difficulties in managing these diseases. Heart disease, adult-onset diabetes, high blood pressure, and food allergies are more common in food insecure households even when factors such as age, sex, income, and education are taken into account. Additionally, food insecurity produces stress and feelings of uncertainty that have health-threatening effects.

Malnutrition during childhood has long-term effects on a child's physiological and psychological development. Often mothers try to protect their children from the nutritional effects of food insecurity by cutting back their own food intake to allow their children to have an adequate diet.

However, try as they may, parents are often unable to protect their children from the negative psychological impacts of household food insecurity. Increasing numbers of studies indicate that children in food insecure households are more likely to experience a whole range of behavioural, emotional, and academic problems than children living in food secure households.

In addition, household food insecurity is also an excellent predictor of Canadians reporting poor or fair health as compared to good, very good, or excellent health. Food insecure individuals are more likely to report having heart disease, adult-onset diabetes, mood/anxiety disorders and a range of other problems (Figure 8.2). The worse the food insecurity, the greater likelihood of poor health. Severely food insecure Canadian adults in Ontario are more than twice as likely to die within four years than food secure Canadians.

Almost always, food insecurity is caused by lack of economic resources. Food banks provide last resort support to food insecure households and exist as a consequence of failed public policies. The majority of food banks in Canada assist clients once per month and in March of 2019, there were 1,084,386 visits to food banks in Canada. Well-meaning efforts to provide food to food insecure families (e.g.,

feeding programs, food banks, and charity drives, etc.) may be making the situation worse by giving the mistaken impression that food insecurity is being dealt with. Therefore, public policies that reduce poverty are the best means of reducing food insecurity.

Policy Implications

• Governments must reduce food insecurity by increasing minimum wages and social assistance rates to the level where an adequate diet is affordable.

• Governments have to assure that healthy foods are affordable (e.g., milk, fruits, and foods high in fiber).

• Providing affordable housing and childcare would reduce other family expenses and leave more money for acquiring an adequate diet.

• Facilitating mothers' employment through job supports, making available affordable childcare, and providing employment training would serve to reduce food insecurity among the most vulnerable Canadian families.

• Better monitoring systems must be designed and implemented to produce up-to-date accounts of food insecurity in Canada.

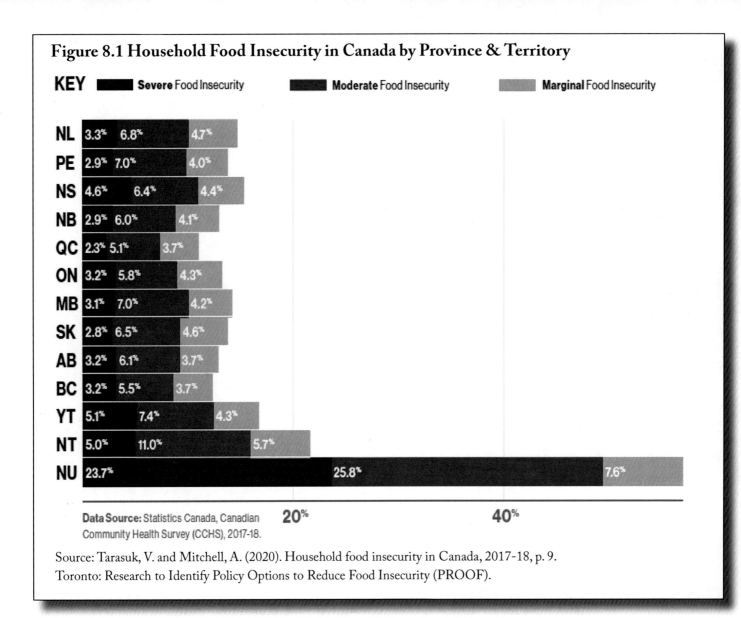

Figure 8.1 Household Food Insecurity in Canada by Province & Territory

KEY ■ **Severe** Food Insecurity ■ **Moderate** Food Insecurity ▨ **Marginal** Food Insecurity

Province/Territory	Severe	Moderate	Marginal
NL	3.3%	6.8%	4.7%
PE	2.9%	7.0%	4.0%
NS	4.6%	6.4%	4.4%
NB	2.9%	6.0%	4.1%
QC	2.3%	5.1%	3.7%
ON	3.2%	5.8%	4.3%
MB	3.1%	7.0%	4.2%
SK	2.8%	6.5%	4.6%
AB	3.2%	6.1%	3.7%
BC	3.2%	5.5%	3.7%
YT	5.1%	7.4%	4.3%
NT	5.0%	11.0%	5.7%
NU	23.7%	25.8%	7.6%

20%   40%

Data Source: Statistics Canada, Canadian Community Health Survey (CCHS), 2017-18.

Source: Tarasuk, V. and Mitchell, A. (2020). Household food insecurity in Canada, 2017-18, p. 9.
Toronto: Research to Identify Policy Options to Reduce Food Insecurity (PROOF).

Figure 8.2 Prevalence of Selected Chronic Conditions among Canadian Adults by Household Food Insecurity Status, 2007-2008

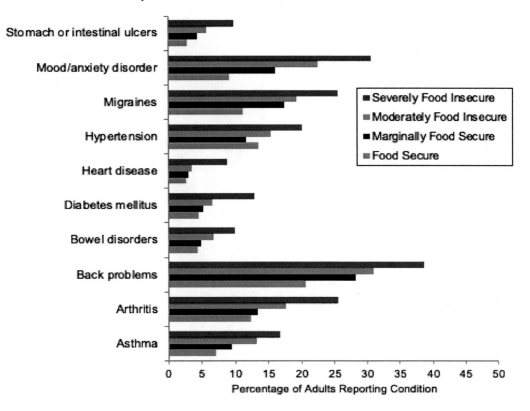

Source: Adapted from Tarasuk V, Mitchell A, McLaren L, & McIntyre L. (2013). Chronic physical and mental health conditions among adults may increase vulnerability to household food insecurity. Journal of Nutrition. 143(11), 1785-93.

Key sources

Food Banks Canada (2019). Hunger Count 2019 Report. Toronto: Author.

Gundersen, C., Tarasuk, V., Cheng, J., De Oliveira, C., & Kurdyak, P. (2018). Food insecurity status and mortality among adults in Ontario, Canada. PloS one, 13(8), e0202642.

Mendly-Zambo, Z. and Raphael, D. (2019). Competing discourses of household food insecurity in Canada. Social Policy and Society, 18 (4), 535-554.

McIntyre, L., & Anderson, L. (2016). Food insecurity. In D. Raphael (Ed.), Social Determinants of Health: Canadian Perspectives, 3rd edition (pp. 294-320). Toronto: Canadian Scholars' Press.

Tarasuk, V. and Mitchell, A. (2020). Household Food Insecurity in Canada, 2017-18. Toronto: Research to Identify Policy Options to Reduce Food Insecurity (PROOF).

Tarasuk, V. (2016). Health implications of food insecurity. In D. Raphael (Ed.), Social Determinants of Health: Canadian Perspectives, 3rd edition (pp. 321-342). Toronto: Canadian Scholars' Press.

9. HOUSING

It would hardly seem necessary to argue the case that housing—and homelessness in particular— are health issues, yet surprisingly few Canadian studies have considered it as such.

– Toba Bryant, 2016

Why Is It Important?

Many studies show that poor quality housing and homelessness are clear threats to the health of Canadians. Housing is an absolute necessity for living a healthy life and living in unsafe, unaffordable or insecure housing increases the risk of many health problems. Lack of economic resources is the prime reason many Canadians experience housing problems. It is also a result of Canadian public policy that has reduced public spending on affordable housing. Canada has generally preferred the market to build, distribute and support the housing stock. This approach renders housing out of reach for modest and low-income households.

Housing is a public policy issue because governments have a responsibility to provide citizens with the prerequisites of health. Canada is signatory to numerous international human rights agreements that guarantee the provision of shelter. Canada is routinely identified by international authorities as not fulfilling these commitments (Figure 9.1).

Housing influences health in many ways. People experience qualitatively different material environments depending on their housing quality. Overcrowding allows for transmission of respiratory and other illnesses. Some Canadian homes, especially on Indigenous reserves, lack clean water and basic sanitation – a fundamental public health risk and are overcrowded. Housing provides a platform for self-expression and identity. High housing costs reduce the resources available to provide other social determinants of health. Living in poor housing creates stress and unhealthy means of coping such as substance abuse.

The presence of lead and mold, poor heating and draft, inadequate ventilation, vermin, and overcrowding are all determinants of adverse health outcomes. Children living in poor quality housing conditions have a greater likelihood of poor health outcomes during childhood as well as adults. Dampness, for example, causes respiratory illness and makes pre-existing health conditions worse. It is not easy to separate the effects of housing from other factors since poverty, poor housing and pre-existing illnesses often go together. Studies that have separated them show poor housing conditions to be an independent cause of adverse health outcomes across the life course.

Canada is experiencing a housing crisis. Over the past 30 years, rents have risen well beyond the cost of living and this is especially so in cities. The term core housing need captures the essence of housing insecurity—a precursor to homelessness. It has three criteria, any one of which identifies core housing need: affordability, in which the household spends 30 percent or more of their income on shelter costs; suitability means that housing is inappropriate for the size and composition of a household—for example, insufficient space for household size (overcrowding); and adequacy, in which the housing requires major repairs, such as those related to plumbing, or it has structural damage.

The 2016 Census found that 12.7 percent of all Canadians were in core housing need with 19.1 percent in Toronto, 17.6 percent in Vancouver and 10.9 percent in Montreal. Renters constitute 47 percent of households in Toronto, 53 percent of households in Vancouver and 63 percent of households in Montreal and their affordability situation is particularly problematic. In Toronto, 47 percent of renters are paying >30 percent of their income on housing and 23 percent are paying more than 50 percent (indicating imminent homelessness) of their income on housing. For Vancouver the figures are 44 percent and 23 percent respectively, and for Montreal, 36 percent and 18 percent respectively.

Most low-income Canadians are among the one-third of Canadians who are renters and rents are increasing faster than renter household incomes. Little new non-profit or co-operative housing have been created since the national program to fund new affordable homes was cancelled in the 1990s. Housing is a mental health concern for the majority of Canadians and this is especially the case for renters (Figure 9.2). Ninety percent of renters, 72 percent of homeowners, and 78 percent of all Canadians believe "It is important the federal government we elect makes improving housing affordability a priority."

A homelessness emergency exists in many Canadian cities. Homeless people experience a much greater rate of a wide range of physical and mental health problems than the general population. Likelihood of early death among homeless people is 8-10 times greater than for the general population.

Contributing factors to the crisis are lack of affordable rental accommodation and growth of part-time and precarious employment that are both low paying and insecure. Canada has one of the highest levels of low-paying jobs at 22 percent and among the highest family poverty rates among Western nations. The result is increasing numbers of families and individuals with insecure housing. Growing numbers of Canadians are under-housed, living in motels, dependent on the shelter system, or living on the street.

Housing insecurity is linked to income insecurity which, in turn, leads to illness and premature death. "Three Cities" research by Dr. David Hulchanski and colleagues at the University of Toronto find that housing and income insecurity, racial identity, and health status are linked in Canada's largest city. They are likely similarly linked in other urban areas.

In late 2017, the federal government released a national housing strategy, but delayed its implementation for one year. The plan identifies a number of housing initiatives to address the needs of different populations and areas of the housing system. The report does not identify what works or what is not working. It provides some new funds to address some urgent needs, but does little to address the weaker features of the housing system.

Housing policy must support non-profit and co-operative housing sectors that have been successful in providing mixed income, and quality affordable housing in existing neighbourhoods. These sectors have been in decline in Canada and other nations, but were very successful in providing secure and affordable housing beginning in the mid-1970s.

Policy Implications

• Housing policy needs to be more explicitly linked to comprehensive income programs (including a jobs strategy), public health, and health services policy.

• The Federation of Canadian Municipalities (FCM) recommends boosting access to social and affordable housing for low-income Canadians.

• FCM also calls for maintaining the funding levels and priorities of the National Housing Strategy, while addressing key gaps.

• The federal government must increase funding for social housing programs targeted for low-income Canadians. Housing policies should support mixed housing as an antidote for urban segregation.

Key sources

BC Non-Profit Housing Association (2020). The Canadian Rental Housing Index. Available at http://rentalhousingindex.ca/en/#intro.

Bryant, T. (2016). Housing and health. In D. Raphael (Ed.), Social Determinants of Health: Canadian Perspectives, 3rd edition (pp. 360-383). Toronto: Canadian Scholars' Press.

Bryant, T. and Shapcott, M. (2016). Housing. In D. Raphael (Ed.), Social Determinants of Health: Canadian Perspectives, 3rd edition (pp. 343-359). Toronto: Canadian Scholars' Press.

Canada Mortgage and Housing Corporation (2020). Understanding Core Housing Need. Ottawa: Author. Available at https://www.cmhc-schl.gc.ca/en/data-and-research/core-housing-need

Chisholm, S. and Hulchanski, D. (2019). Canada's housing story. In D. Maclennan, H. Pawson, K. Gibb, S. Chisholm & D. Hulchanski (Eds.), Shaping Futures: Changing the Housing Story: Final Report. Glasgow: Policy Scotland, University of Glasgow.

Hulchanski, D. (2019). How Segregated is Toronto? Inequality, Polarization, and Segregation Trends and Processes. Available at https://www.ryerson.ca/content/dam/rcis/documents/Segregation_Trends_in_Toronto_Hulchanski_at_Ryerson_14_Feb_2019_w_Appendix.pdf

Figure 9.1 UN Rapporteur on Housing Chides Canadian Government over Need for Rights-Based Approach to Housing

"Widespread homelessness and lack of access to adequate housing, in so affluent a country as Canada is clearly one of the most critical human rights issues facing all levels of government. Rights-based legislation must establish mechanisms for those affected to raise systemic issues regarding the progressive realization of the right to housing and ensure that governments will respond by implementing remedies... It must also include measures to eliminate the deep disparities in access to adequate, affordable, safe, and secure housing for Indigenous peoples, women, members of racialized communities, persons with disabilities, trans and gender-diverse people, older adults, children and young people, migrants, refugees, asylum-seekers and stateless persons."

Source: Leilani Farha, UN Special Rapporteur on the Right to Adequate Housing. Open Letter on the Right to Housing to Prime Minister Trudeau, August 14, 2018. Available at http://nhs.socialrights.ca/wp-content/uploads/2018/08/Open-Letter-to-Prime-Minister-Trudeau.pdf

Figure 9.2 Housing is a Mental Health Issue for Many Canadians

CANADIANS: HOUSING & FINANCIAL STRESS IN THE LAST 12 MONTHS

My finances were my biggest source of stress at least once:

ALL RESPONDENTS	79%
HOMEOWNERS	75%
RENTERS	86%

Dealing with rising housing costs negatively impacted my mental health at least once:

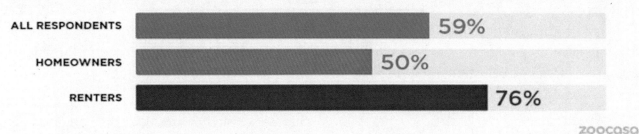

ALL RESPONDENTS	59%
HOMEOWNERS	50%
RENTERS	76%

zoocasa

Source: Zoocasa (2019). 84% of Canadians Feel Housing Affordability is a Major Issue: National Survey. Available at https://www.zoocasa.com/blog/zoocasa-national-housing-survey-2019/

10. SOCIAL EXCLUSION

Social exclusion is manifest through forms of oppression that order institutional arrangements and power relations with the effect of marginalizing particular groups in society.

– Grace-Edward Galabuzi, 2016

Why Is It Important?

Social exclusion refers to specific groups being denied the opportunity to participate in Canadian life. In Canada, Indigenous Canadians, Canadians of colour, recent immigrants, low income Canadians, women, and people with disabilities are especially likely to experience social exclusion. Many aspects of Canadian society marginalize people and limit their access to social, cultural and economic resources. Socially excluded Canadians are more likely to be unemployed and earn lower wages. They have less access to health and social services and means of furthering their education. These groups are increasingly being segregated into specific neighborhoods. Excluded groups have little influence upon decisions made by governments and other institutions. They lack power.

There are four aspects to social exclusion. Denial of participation in civil affairs is a result of legal sanction and other institutional mechanisms. Laws and regulations prevent non-status residents or immigrants from participation in a range of activities. Systemic forms of discrimination based on race, gender, ethnicity or disability status, excludes people. New Canadians are frequently unable to practice their professions due to a myriad of regulations and procedures that bar their participation. Denial of social goods such as health care, education, housing, income security, and language services is common. Socially excluded

groups earn lower incomes than Canadians. They also lack affordable housing and experience less access to services.

Exclusion from social production is a lack of opportunity to participate and contribute to social and cultural activities. Much of this results from the lack of financial resources that facilitate involvement. Economic exclusion is when individuals cannot access economic resources and opportunities such as participation in paid work. All of these forms of exclusion are common to Indigenous Canadians, Canadians of colour, recent immigrants, women, and people with disabilities. Low income Canadians of every type lack the financial means to fully participate in Canadian life.

The specific situations of immigrants, Indigenous Canadians, Canadians of colour, persons with disabilities, and women are considered in later sections of this document.

Social exclusion creates the living conditions and personal experiences that endanger health. Social exclusion also creates a myriad of educational and social problems. Social exclusion creates a sense of powerlessness, hopelessness and depression that further diminish the possibilities of inclusion in society.

The presence of social exclusion and its impact upon health is dramatically illustrated in Figure 10.1. Maps of neighbourhoods in the City of Toronto are provided that detail the varying concentrations of poverty, diabetes, and visible minorities in these neighbourhoods. The correspondence among poverty rates, prevalence of diabetes, and concentration of visible minorities is striking. COVID-19 incidence and hospitalization rates in Toronto mirror these findings.

These findings are consistent with studies that find that marginalization and exclusion of individuals and communities from mainstream society constitute a primary factor leading to adult-onset diabetes and a range of other chronic diseases such as respiratory and cardiovascular disease. Social exclusion is also related to a range of social problems that include educational underachievement and crime.

It appears that the restructuring of Canada's economy and labour market toward flexible labour markets has served to accelerate these processes of social exclusion. The quality of jobs is increasingly stratified along racial lines, with a disproportionate proportion of low-income sector employment being taken by Canadians of colour and recent immigrants.

Similarly, outside of health care and elementary and secondary education, Canadian governments provide few universal programs and benefits as compared to many other wealthy nations. Social exclusion is increasing therefore as a result of increasing precariousness of employment, the fact that these precarious jobs are increasingly being filled by minority Canadians, and Canada's lack of universal programs and benefits that enable greater participation in Canadian society.

Source (Figure 10.1):
Monsebraaten, L. and Daly, R. (November 1, 2007). Diabetes Lurks in Urban Sprawl. Toronto: Toronto Star. Available at https://www.pressreader.com/canada/toronto-star/20071101/page/1

Policy Implications

•   Governments at all levels must revise laws and regulations that will address growing precarious and low wage employment in Canada.

•   Governments must enforce laws that protect the rights of minority groups, particularly concerning employment rights and anti-discrimination.

•   The tax structure needs to be revised to increase progressivity to allow governments to provide greater benefits and supports to all Canadians. These include affordable housing, childcare, and pharmacare, and other benefits such as employment training that are provided in many other wealthy nations.

Key sources

CBC News (2020). Lower income people, new immigrants at higher COVID-19 risk in Toronto, data suggests. Available at https://www.cbc.ca/news/canada/toronto/low-income-immigrants-covid-19-infection-1.5566384

Galabuzi, G. E. (2016). Social exclusion. In Raphael, D. (Ed.), Social Determinants of Health: Canadian Perspectives, 3rd edition (pp. 388-418). Toronto: Canadian Scholars' Press.

Noël, A. (2012). Fighting Poverty, Inequalities, and Social Exclusion: Conference Report. Montreal: QICSS and CRDCN. Available at https://crdcn.org/sites/default/files/final_conference_report.pdf.

Raphael D. (2020) Making sense of poverty: Social inequality and social exclusion. In: Raphael, D. (Ed.) Poverty in Canada: Implications for Health and Quality of Life, 3rd edition, (pp. 87-117). Toronto: Canadian Scholars' Press.

White, P. (1998). Ideologies, social exclusion and spatial segregation in Paris. In S. Musterd & W. Ostendorf (Eds.), Urban Segregation and the Welfare State: Inequality and Exclusion in Western Cities (pp. 148-167). London, UK: Routledge.

Figure 10.1 Poverty, Diabetes, and Visible Minorities in Toronto

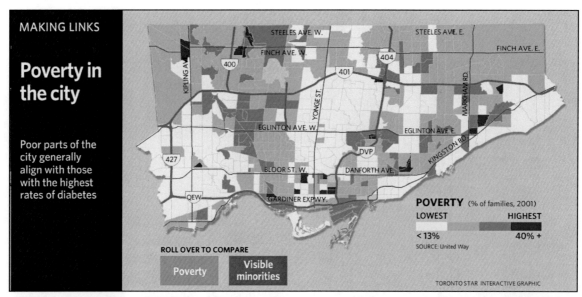

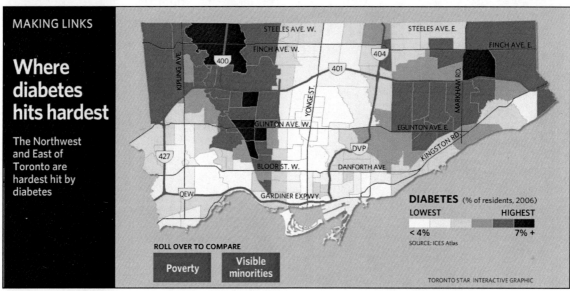

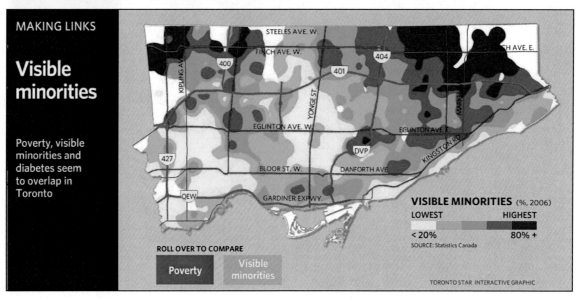

11. SOCIAL SAFETY NET

Canadians are experiencing rising inequality due to a host of policy changes by federal and provincial governments, policies that not only eroded the social safety net erected by the welfare state in previous decades, but contributed to a fundamental alteration in the role and scope of the state.

– David Langille, 2016

Why Is It Important?

The social safety net refers to a range of benefit programs and supports that protect citizens during various life changes that can affect their health. These life changes include normal life transitions such as having and raising children, attaining education or employment training, seeking housing, entering the labour force, and reaching retirement.

There are also unexpected life events such as having an accident, experiencing family break-ups, becoming unemployed, and developing a physical or mental illness or disability that makes one unable to work. The primary way these events threaten health is that they increase economic insecurity and provoke psychological stress, all important determinants of health.

In Canada, becoming unable to work through unemployment or illness and experiencing family break-ups are good predictors of coming to experience poverty. These events are usually outside of an individual's control. All wealthy nations have created systems – usually termed the welfare state – to offer protection and supports to its citizens to help deal with these threats. These include family allowances, childcare, unemployment insurance, health and social services, social assistance and disability benefits and supports, home care and retirement pensions.

The protections and supports offered by Canadian governments are well below those provided by most other wealthy nations (Figures 11.1 and 11.2). Employment Insurance is available in Canada for only 45 weeks. After that, a person can receive social assistance benefits only if they are virtually destitute with no liquid funds.

The Organisation for Economic Co-operation and Development (OECD) publishes extensive statistics on social safety net spending among its 36 member nations. Canada ranks 24th of 36 countries and spends only 17.3 percent of gross domestic product (GDP) on social expenditures. Among OECD countries, Canada is among the lowest public spenders on family benefits (25th of 36), seniors' pensions (30th of 36), social assistance payments (26th of 33 nations for which data is available), unemployment benefits (19th of 36), and benefits and services for people with disabilities (32nd of 36).

As one example of Canada's frayed social safety net, employment insurance is available to people who are without employment and who meet the eligibility requirements. Recent changes to eligibility, however, have significantly reduced the percentage of Canadians who are eligible for such payments. Of the 1.1 million Canadians unemployed in 2018,

63.9 percent had contributed to the program and of these 87.4 percent had accumulated enough hours. In essence, only 55.8 percent of unemployed Canadian were entitled to benefits.

A well-functioning social safety net is not only about providing financial benefits. It also includes services such as counseling, employment training and community services. For instance, active labour policy refers to supporting unemployed citizens by providing training opportunities and resources for finding new jobs. Canada ranks 28th of 36 OECD countries on such spending. Volunteer-based activities and peer support offer a valuable extension of social safety net provision by Canadian governments. However, voluntary action cannot eliminate the need for basic security and protection provided by governmental institutions.

Canadian citizens require protection when markets fail to provide basic security and adequate income. Sole reliance on the private market system increases insecurity among the population. A weak social safety net turns citizen against communal action and decreases social cohesion. These have health-threatening effects. Citizens experience better physical and mental health when they have a secure base for living a productive life.

Policy Implications

• The social safety net provided by Canadian federal, provincial/territorial, and municipal governments needs to be strengthened. Canada's spending in support of citizens lags far behind many other wealthy nations. Current benefits do not provide adequate supports for life transitions.

• Canadian decision-makers must re-evaluate whether minimizing government intervention is an ethical and sustainable approach to maintaining health, promoting social well-being, and increasing economic productivity.

• Strong political and social movements are needed to pressure governments into creating public policy that will strengthen Canada's social safety net.

Key sources

Bryant, T. (2016). Health Policy in Canada, 2nd edition. Toronto: Canadian Scholars' Press.

Hallstrom, L. (2016). Public policy and the welfare state. In D. Raphael (Ed.), Social Determinants of Health: Canadian Perspectives, 3rd edition (pp. 521-490). Toronto: Canadian Scholars' Press.

Langille, D. (2016). Follow the money: How business and politics shape our health. In D. Raphael (Ed.), Social Determinants of Health: Canadian Perspectives, 3rd edition (pp. 470-490). Toronto: Canadian Scholars' Press.

Organisation for Economic Co-operation and Development. (2019). Society at a Glance: OECD Social Indicators 2019 Edition. Paris: Author.

Raphael, D. (2020). Canadian public policy and poverty in international perspective. In D. Raphael, Poverty in Canada: Implications for Health and Quality of Life, 3rd edition (pp. 419-452). Toronto: Canadian Scholars' Press.

Figure 11.1 Unemployment Replacement Rates over Short Term (6 months) [Employment Insurance in Canada] and Long Term (2 years) [Social Assistance in Canada] for Persons Earning 67 Percent of Average Earnings, 2018

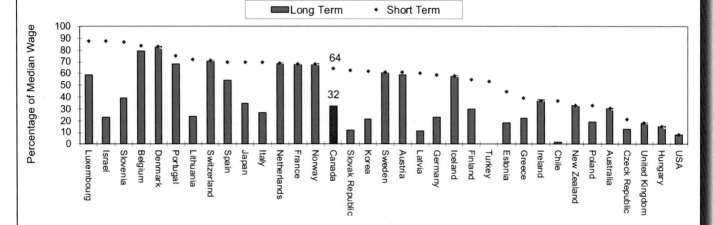

Source: Organisation for Economic Cooperation and Development. (2019). Benefits in unemployment, share of previous income. Available at https://data.oecd.org/benwage/benefits-in-unemployment-share-of-previous-income.htm

Figure 11.2 Average Net Incomes Provided by Social Assistance As Percentage of Median Equivalent Household Income, Couple with Two Children, 2017

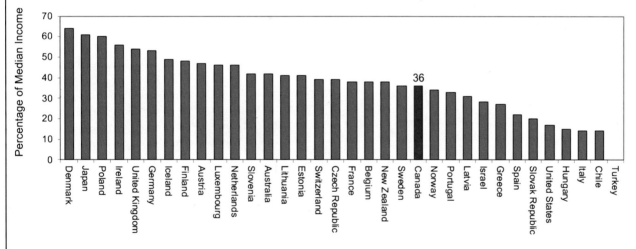

Source: Organisation for Economic Cooperation and Development (2020). Adequacy of guaranteed minimum income benefits. Available at https://stats.oecd.org/Index.aspx?DataSetCode=IA

12. HEALTH SERVICES

The sheer weight of evidence regarding inequities in health outcomes and health care access requires a systems-based and human rights perspective beyond individual biophysical status and genetic endowment.

– Elizabeth McGibbon, 2016

Why Is It Important?

High quality health care services are a social determinant of health as well as a basic human right. The purpose of a universal health care system is to protect the health of citizens and spread health costs across the whole society. A universal health care system is especially effective in protecting citizens with lower incomes who cannot afford private health care insurance.

The Canada Health Act (1984) sets out requirements provincial and territorial governments must meet through their public health-care insurance plans. These are: public administration, comprehensiveness, universality, portability, and accessibility. The "single payer" concept describes the concept of health care administration by a public authority (public administration).

The Canada Health Act requires provinces and territories provide all "medically necessary" services on a universal basis (comprehensiveness). All residents are provided access to public health-care insurance on equal terms and conditions (universality). However, provincial and territorial governments have great discretionary power because the Act does not provide a detailed list of insured services. Therefore, the range of insured services varies among provinces and territories.

Provinces and territories provide health services

to Canadian citizens when they are temporarily absent from their home province or territory or out of country (portability). The Canada Health Act states every Canadian has to be provided uniform access to health services in a way that is free of financial barriers (accessibility). No one should be discriminated against on the basis of income, age, or health status.

Nevertheless, there are continuing issues of access to care. The Commonwealth Fund ranked Canada's health care system 9th of 11 wealthy nations (Australia, Canada, France, Germany, Netherlands, New Zealand, Norway, Sweden, Switzerland, the United Kingdom, and the United States). Rankings were based on clusters of ratings for care process (Canada ranked 6th), access (10th), administrative efficiency (6th), equity (9th), and health care outcomes (9th).

More specifically, in regard to issues of affordability, 30 percent of Canadian doctors reported their patients often had difficulty paying for medications or out-of-pocket costs. Twenty-eight percent of patients reporting skipping dental check-ups or care because of costs over the previous year and 16 percent of Canadians reported having cost-related access problems to medical care in that time.

In relation to timeliness, 63 percent of Canadians reported that it was somewhat or very difficult to obtain after-hours care and 50 percent reported having to wait two hours or more for care in emergency rooms. Forty percent of doctors reported their patients often experienced difficulty getting specialized tests and 30 percent of patients reported having to wait two months or longer for specialist appointments.

The equity indicators look at differences between individuals with above-average versus those with below-average income. There was a 24 percent difference between above- and below-average-income Canadians in regard to skipping dental care or check-ups because of cost in the past year. There was a 9 percent difference regarding whether their regular doctor spent enough time with them to explain things. There was a 19 percent difference in having cost-related access problems with medical care in the past year and an 8 percent difference in being able to obtain after-hours care. In every case, the above-average-income Canadians had greater access to care than below-average Canadians.

There are also issues related to coverage. Canada's medicare system ranks 13th highest on health care spending at 7.5 percent of GDP, but only covers 73 percent of health care costs – the rest is covered by private insurance plans and out-of-pocket spending – giving it a rank of 21st of 36 nations (Figures 12.1 and 12.2). Medicare does not cover drug costs, and coverage of home care and nursing costs varies among provinces and territories. In many other wealthy nations these costs are covered by the public health care system.

Canadians with below-average incomes are three times less likely to fill a prescription due to cost. While a pharmacare program has long been recommended by Royal Commissions for its promoting health and controlling costs, it has not been put into practice. Drug costs accounted for 14 percent of total health expenditures in 2017 and are the third largest expenditure. Hospital and physician costs are first and second. Home care will also become increasingly important with the aging of the population. There is little evidence of reform in this area as well.

Dental insurance plans are available to only 26 percent of the lowest income groups of Canadians and to 77 percent of the highest income groups. Not surprisingly, lower income Canadians were much more likely to see dental costs as a burden, avoid/delay care, and be unable have all needed treatments.

Policy Implications

•   Health authorities and health policy makers must direct attention to existing inequities in access to health care and identify and remove barriers to health care.

•   Governments must implement a pharmacare program and increase public coverage of home care and nursing home costs.

•   The medicare system must be strengthened and governments should resist the increasing involvement of for-profit companies in the organization and delivery of health care.

•   Health authorities must find means of controlling the use of costly but ineffective new treatments (e.g., pharmaceuticals and screening technologies) that are being marketed aggressively by private corporations.

•   Consideration should be given to providing dental care to families living on low incomes.

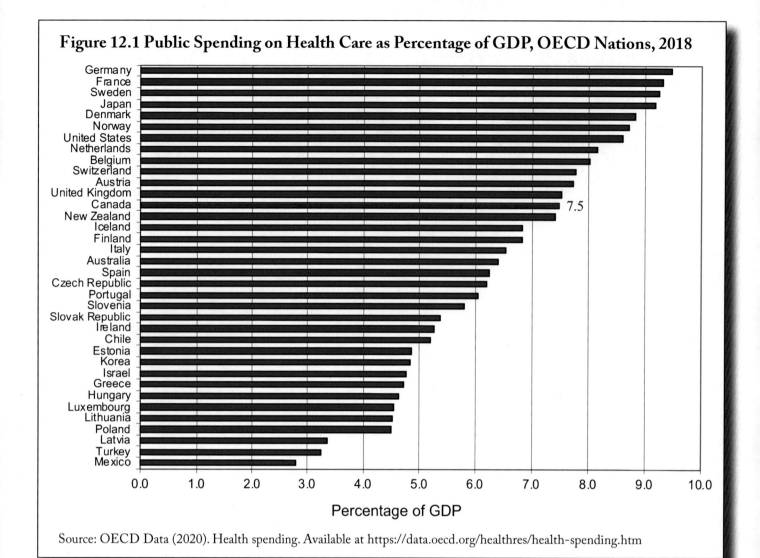

Figure 12.1 Public Spending on Health Care as Percentage of GDP, OECD Nations, 2018

Source: OECD Data (2020). Health spending. Available at https://data.oecd.org/healthres/health-spending.htm

Figure 12.2 Public Spending on Health Care as Percentage of Total Health Care Spending, OECD Nations, 2017

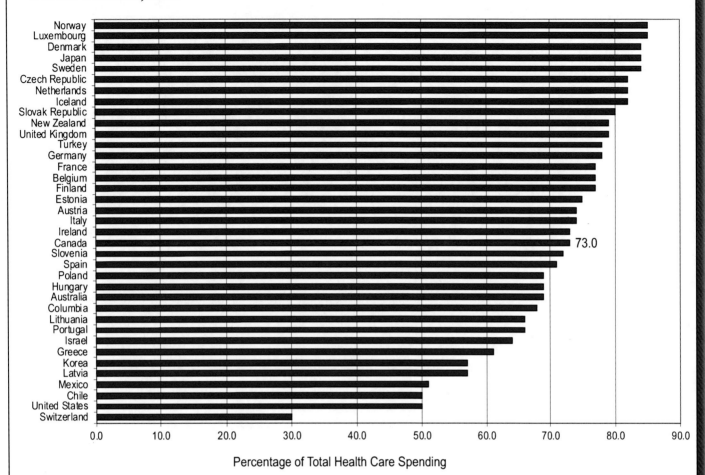

Percentage of Total Health Care Spending

Source: OECD Data (2020). Health spending. Available at https://data.oecd.org/healthres/health-spending.htm

Key sources

Bryant, T. (2016). Health Policy in Canada, 2nd edition. Toronto: Canadian Scholars' Press.

McGibbon, E. (2016). Oppressions and access to health care: Deepening the conversation. In D. Raphael (Ed.), Social Determinants of Health: Canadian Perspectives, 3rd edition (pp. 491-520). Toronto: Canadian Scholars' Press.

Raphael, D. (2020). Interactions with the health and social services sectors. In D. Raphael (Ed.), Poverty in Canada: Implications for Health and Quality of Life, 3rd edition (pp. 187-224). Toronto: Canadian Scholars' Press.

Raphael D. (2019) Narrative review of affinities and differences between the social determinants of oral and general health in Canada: Establishing a common agenda. Journal of Public Health 41: e218–e225.

Schneider, E. C., Sarnak, D. O, Squires, D., et al. (2017). Mirror, Mirror 2017: International Comparison Reflects Flaws and Opportunities for Better US Health Care. Available at https://www.commonwealthfund.org/publications/fund-reports/2017/jul/mirror-mirror-2017-international-comparison-reflects-flaws-and.

13. GEOGRAPHY

Geography and health are intrinsically linked. Where we are born, live, study and work directly influence our health experiences: the air we breathe, the food we eat, the viruses we are exposed to and the health services we can access.

– Trevor J.B. Dummer, 2008

Why Is It Important?

Geography most obviously influences our health through the air we breath, the food and water we consume, and the environmental pollution and vectors of disease to which we are exposed. In addition, rural, remote, isolated, Northern and urban geographies determine not only physical aspects of the environment, but also other social determinant of health such as access to health care, food, education, employment and housing, among others, that directly shape our health.

Encompassing more than simply space and location, geography also involves how humans organize themselves and create "places". Geography illuminates interrelations between land, space, territory and human experiences that are themselves shaped by socio-political and economic dimensions of society. While the average life expectancy for Canada is 84.0 years for women and 79.9 years for men, in British Columbia it is 84.6 years for women and 80.1 years for men, yet in the territory of Nunavut, where there is a significant proportion of Indigenous people, it is 73.4 years for women and 70.8 years for men.

Numerous studies show associations between health and the geographies of urban versus rural life. Death rates from treatable diseases are related to geographical remoteness, with rates significantly

higher for 'remote' and 'very remote' areas, especially for males (Figure 13.1).

Geography also create specific vulnerabilities and health risks in both rural and urban areas which are largely avoidable. For example, public policies that create housing insecurity intersect with racial discrimination and urban ghettoization directed towards recent immigrants of colour. Additionally, gentrification of urban areas deepens disadvantage for immigrant and communities of colour across local geographies. The map below (Figure 13.2) plots marginalization index scores across Toronto neighbourhoods, showing pockets of marginalization in the inner city and on the outskirts of Toronto where immigrant and racialized communities tend to settle.

Even more specifically, public policy regulations concerning environmental protections and urban planning determine locations of toxic waste dumps, levels of air and water pollution, and other types of environmental contamination that shape health. Geography becomes an important determinant for those risks, as racism, colonialism and oppression enable the location of toxic waste sites, landfills and incinerators to be in close proximity to communities of colour, poor neighbourhoods and Indigenous lands.

Geography as a determinant of health is especially important for its impact on Indigenous people's health. De Leeuw argues for a geographic lens for understanding the health of Indigenous people. In addition, the lesson from Indigenous cosmologies, where the physical geography of the world is understood as intrinsic to human wellbeing, needs to be learned by policymakers. In the words of prominent Indigenous scholar Robin Wall Kimmerer: "[w]e make a grave error if we try to separate individual well-being from the health of the whole."

Finally, the climate crisis is a glaring illustration of the importance of geography as it changes landscapes through the erosion of coastal areas, severe floods, draughts and massive wildfires, making land unsuitable for human and other species. Geography as a determinant of health within the context of the climate crisis draws attention to the responsibility to live on the Earth within boundaries that limit the destructive activities of humans. This requires a shift in how we conceptualize health, placing it within a holistic model that extends to the health of all species and the environment.

Policy Implications

• Canadian researchers and policymakers must take note of health inequalities related to various geographies existing in Canada.

• More targeted research is needed on the impact of industrial pollution for human and environmental health and its geographical distribution.

• Governments should enact laws that regulate environmental impact of industries and make these industries legally responsible for the health-damaging consequences of their activities.

• Urban planners must consider the ecological impact on cities of the inequitable distribution of resources across urban spaces.

• Health, environmental and policy researchers need to collaborate with Indigenous scholars and frame health holistically whereby the health of humans is connected with the health of the environment and survival of its diversity of species.

Key sources

Dummer, T. J. (2008). Health geography: Supporting public health policy and planning. Canadian Medical Association Journal, 178(9), 1177-1180.

De Leeuw, S. (2018). Activating place: Geography as a determinant of Indigenous peoples' health and wellbeing. In Greenwood, M., de Leeuw, S. and Lindsay, N. (Eds.) Determinants of Indigenous Peoples' Health: Beyond the Social (pp. 187-203). Toronto: Canadian Scholars' Press.

Kimmerer, R. (2013). Braiding Sweetgrass: Indigenous Wisdom, Scientific Knowledge and the Teachings of Plants. Minneapolis: Milkweed Editions.

McGibbon, E. (2016). Oppressions and access to health care: Deepening the conversation. In D. Raphael (Ed.) Social Determinants of Health: Canadian Perspectives, 3rd edition (pp. 491-520). Toronto: Canadian Scholars' Press.

Ontario Community Health Profiles Partnership (2020). Ontario Health Profiles. Toronto: St. Michael's Hospital. Available at http://www.ontariohealthprofiles.ca/

Subedi, R., Greenberg, T. L., & Roshanafshar, S. (2019). Does geography matter in mortality? An analysis of potentially avoidable mortality by remoteness index in Canada. Health Reports, 30, 3-15.

Figure 13.1 Preventable Mortality Rate by Sex and Relative Remoteness

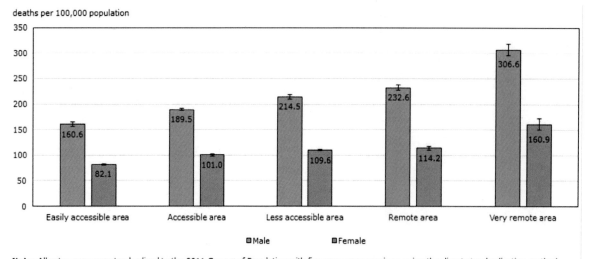

Note: All rates were age standardized to the 2011 Census of Population with five-year age groupings, using the direct standardization method.

Source: Canadian Vital Statistics. Death Database 2011 to 2015 and Remoteness Index.

Figure 13.2 Ontario Marginalization Index. Material Deprivation Quintiles for Toronto Neighbouhoods, 2016.

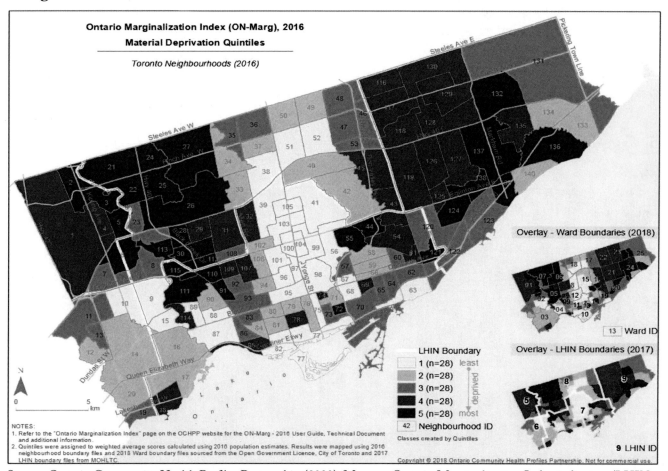

Source: Ontario Community Health Profiles Partnership (2020). Maps — Ontario Marginalization Index indicators (LHIN 7 Neighbourhoods). Available at https://tinyurl.com/yytrgmf2

14. DISABILITY

As a highly-developed nation, Canada still lags behind in the implementation of its obligations under the Convention on the Rights of Persons with Disabilities. There are significant shortcomings in the way the federal, provincial and territorial governments of Canada respect, protect and fulfill the rights of persons with disabilities.

– Catalina Devandas-Aguilar, 2019

Why Is It Important?

Too often disability is seen in medical rather than societal terms. While disability is clearly related to physical and mental functioning, the primary issue is whether society is willing to provide persons with disabilities with the supports and opportunities necessary to participate in Canadian life. As compared to the other wealthy developed nations of the OECD, Canada's levels of benefits to persons with disabilities are very low, and its support for integration of persons with disabilities into society is below the OECD average.

The percentage of Canadians reporting a disability is 22.3 percent. Among youth aged 15-24 years, the rate is 13.1 percent, but for adults aged 25 to 64 years, the rate rises to 20 percent. For those aged 65 and over, the rate is 38 percent. Women (24 percent) are more likely to have a disability than men (20 percent). This gender difference occurs across all age groups.

People with disabilities are less likely to be employed and, when they are employed, earn less than people without disabilities. Only 59 percent of Canadians with disabilities aged 25 to 64 are employed compared to 80 percent of Canadians without disabilities. Severity of disability is related to employment: it is 76 percent for those with mild disabilities, but only 31 percent for those with very severe disabilities. Persons with disabilities earn less than Canadians without disabilities (12 percent less for those with milder disabilities and 51 percent less for those with more severe disabilities) and are more likely to live in poverty.

Of those 80 percent of Canadians without a disability who are employed, 92.5 percent of men and 81.2 percent of women work full time. Of the much fewer 59 percent of persons with disabilities who are employed, only 89.2 percent of men with milder disabilities were employed full-time while the figure for those with more severe disabilities was 74.9 percent. For women with mild disabilities, 77.2 percent were working full time and for those with more severe disabilities, 70.9 percent were working full time.

More troubling, the rate of unemployment is 24 percent for those with mild disabilities and a whopping 69 percent for those with very severe disabilities. Among working age adults, aged 25 to 64 years, personal income was strongly related to the severity of disability.

Those without disabilities had a higher median personal after-tax income ($38,980) than those with milder disabilities ($34,330) and those with more severe disabilities ($19,160). In fact, the income of those with more severe disabilities was half that of those with no disabilities. Not surprisingly, the poverty rate (LIM-AT) for Canadians without disabilities was 8.6 percent in 2014, but 23.2 percent for those with a disability.

Since over 40 percent of Canadians with disabilities are not in the labour force, many have to rely upon social assistance benefits. These benefits are very low in Canada and do not bring individuals even close to the poverty line in most cities. This should not be surprising as Canada is one of the most frugal OECD nations in its allocation of benefits to people with disabilities. The OECD calculates spending on disability-related cash benefits as well as spending on efforts to support participation of those with disabilities in the labour market. Canada ranks 32nd of 36 OECD nations in these kinds of spending (Figure 14.1).

In 2004, the OECD carried out an extensive analysis of disability policy in its member nations. It created indices of compensation and integration for persons with disabilities. Each index consisted of ten measures of the extent to which governments provide benefits and supports to persons with disabilities. Canada, outside of Korea, provided the lowest compensations and benefits to its citizens with disabilities. Canada also had some of the strongest restrictions on receiving benefits and its levels of benefits were very low. Canada did somewhat better – but still fell below the OECD average – in efforts to integrate persons with disabilities into the workforce.

There is little reason to think much has changed since then. In 2007, Canada spent only .9 percent of GDP on disability-related benefits. In 2017, the figure declined to .8 percent of GDP. Figure 14.2 shows the situation in Canada and 18 other OECD nations from 1990-2014. Among the nations included, Canada spent the lowest on compensation and was below most on integration spending. Clearly, there is much work to be done in assisting persons with disabilities in Canada.

Many employment issues are related to the workplace being either unable or unwilling to accommodate to the needs of persons with disabilities. Many required modifications are rather minor and almost all of these would have annual costs of less than $2,000. For many persons with disabilities, an employer's reluctance to provide accommodation on the job can be extremely disheartening and frustrating.

Canada ratified the UN Convention on the Rights of Persons with Disabilities and therefore is now required to report on its progress in improving the situation. In 2017, the UN Committee on the Rights of Persons with Disabilities provided critical concluding observations on the initial report of Canada. Key recommendations by the Special Rapporteur on the Rights of Persons with Disabilities are provided in the policy implications below. The Disability Rights Promotion International website provides further information on the Convention and its implications at http://www.yorku.ca/drpi.

Policy Implications

• Since there is no national policy in Canada to coordinate and guide the implementation of the CRPD at the national, federal, provincial or territory levels, Canada should commit to appoint an independent monitoring mechanism as required by article 33 (2) of the Convention to promote, protect and monitor its implementation.

• Discussions about the rights of persons with disabilities should move beyond framing it in terms of social assistance to one that takes a human rights-based approach.

- Institute provincial and territorial policies that provide fully inclusive education systems since it is lacking in many provinces and territories.

- Canada should review its social protection system to ensure rights-based responses that promote the active citizenship, social inclusion and community participation of persons with disabilities.

- Canada must implement comprehensive public policies that guarantee the access of persons with disabilities to the support they need to live independently in their communities.

Key sources

Böheim, R., & Leoni, T. (2018). Sickness and disability policies: Reform paths in OECD countries between 1990 and 2014. International Journal of Social Welfare, 27(2), 168-185.

Organisation for Economic Co-operation and Development (OECD) (2003). Transforming Disability into Ability. Paris: Author.

Morris, S., Fawcett, G., Brisebois, L. and Hughes, J. (2018). A Demographic, Employment and Income Profile of Canadians with Disabilities Aged 15 Years and Over, 2017. Ottawa: Statistics Canada. Available at https://www150.statcan.gc.ca/n1/en/pub/89-654-x/89-654-x2018002-eng.pdf?st=jhnnVQX-

Rioux, M. and Daly, T. (2019). Constructing disability and illness. In T. Bryant, D. Raphael, and M. Rioux (Eds.). Staying Alive: Critical Perspectives on Health, Illness, and Health Care, 3rd edition (pp. 351-371). Toronto: Canadian Scholars' Press.

United Nations Committee on the Rights of Persons with Disabilities (CRPD) (2017). Concluding Observations on the Initial Report of Canada. New York: Author. Available at https://tinyurl.com/qvmgl55

Wall, K. (2017). Low Income Among Persons with a Disability in Canada. Ottawa: Statistics Canada. Available at https://www150.statcan.gc.ca/n1/pub/75-006-x/2017001/article/54854-eng.htm

Figure 14.1 Public Expenditure on Disability-Related Benefits as % of GDP, OECD Nations, 2017

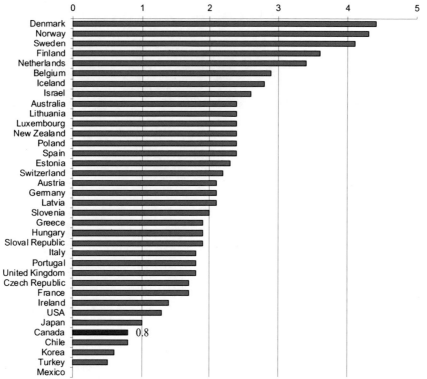

Source: Data from Organisation for Economic Co-operation and Development. (2018). Government Spending on Incapacity. Available at https://data.oecd.org/socialexp/public-spending-on-incapacity.htm#indicator-chart

Figure 14.2 OECD Disability Policy Score Levels, 1990, 2000, 2007 and 2014

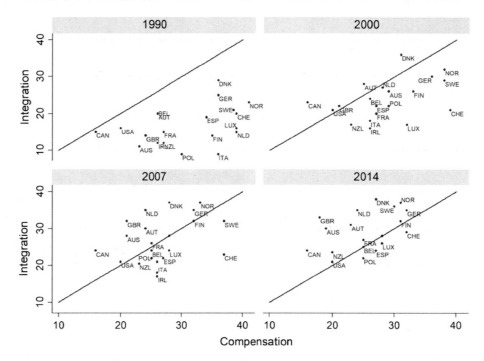

Source: Böheim, R., & Leoni, T. (2018). Sickness and disability policies: Reform paths in OECD countries between 1990 and 2014. International Journal of Social Welfare, 27(2), 168-185.

15. INDIGENOUS ANCESTRY

As one of the richest countries in the world, Canada is well placed to right past wrongs and ensure that all Canadians, including Canada's First Peoples, are able to enjoy living conditions that promote health and well–being.

– Janet Smylie and Michelle Firestone, 2016

Why Is It Important?

Indigenous peoples in Canada number 1,673,785 people, or 4.9 percent of the national population, with 977,230 First Nations people, 587,545 Métis, and 65,025 Inuit. The health of Indigenous peoples in Canada is inextricably tied up with their history of colonialization. This has taken the form of legislation such as the Indian Act of 1876, disregard for land claims of Metis peoples, relocation of Inuit communities, and the establishment of residential schools. The result has been the experience by Indigenous people in Canada of adverse social determinants of health and adverse health outcomes.

The average income of all Indigenous men and women in 2016 was $28,560 and $23,681 respectively, which is 69 percent of the average income of non-Indigenous men ($41,230) and 81 percent of the average income of non-Indigenous women ($29,131). For Indigenous Canadians living on reserves, their respective figures as a percentage of non-Indigenous incomes were for men, 44 percent ($18,483) and for women, 63 percent ($18,483). Figures were somewhat better for those living off reserve (for men, $33,442 or 80 percent of non-Indigenous incomes; for women, $25,006 or 84 percent of non-Indigenous incomes) but still well below incomes of non-Indigenous Canadians.

In 2016, 24 percent of Indigenous Canadians had incomes below the low-income after-tax cut-offs (poverty rate) in contrast to the 14 percent figures for non-Indigenous Canadians. The figures for First Nations peoples were 30 percent; Metis, 17.5 percent; and Inuit, 19 percent. In 2016, the Indigenous unemployment rate was 10.1 percent, almost double the rate of non-Indigenous households of 5.5 percent. For First Nations Canadians living on reserves, the figure was 25 percent, over twice the rate for Indigenous Canadians living off reserve.

Education levels differ widely between Indigenous and other Canadians. In 2016 among First Nations people living on reserve, 52.9 percent of men and 61 percent of women attained high school education. The figures are better for First Nations people living off reserve; 73.2 percent for men and 78.7 percent for women. Figures for Inuit peoples are 55 percent for men and 57.1 percent for women, and for Metis, 78.8 percent for men and 84.8 percent for women. But these figures compare unfavourably to non-Indigenous Canadians where 87.7 percent of men and 90.6 percent of women attained high school education.

In 2017/2018, while the food insecurity rate for all Canadians was 12 percent, it was 28.2 percent for Indigenous Canadians. A 2018 study of 100 randomly selected First Nations communities across Canada found that 48 percent of First Nations households are food insecure. In Alberta 60 percent of Indigenous families were food insecure which is seven times higher than the national food insecurity rate of 8.4 percent. In Nunavut, 57 percent of households are food insecure. Among children in Nunavut, this figure is 78.7 percent.

Ten percent of non-Indigenous households were in core housing need in 2016 (lacking either affordability, suitability, or adequacy). Among Indigenous Canadian the figure was 19.8 percent; for status Indians, 23.9 percent; non-status Indians, 19 percent; Metis, 14.3 percent;and Inuit, 39 percent.

Indigenous people are more than three times more likely to be living in dwellings in need of major repair (23.4 percent) than non-Indigenous Canadians (7 percent). The figures for First Nations Canadians living on reserve are 44.1 percent; for those off-reserve, 13.8 percent; for Inuit, 26.2 percent; and for Metis, 11.3 percent.

The lower incomes of Indigenous Canadians and their higher poverty rates lead to their greater incidence of a range of afflictions and premature death from a variety of causes. While Canada's overall life expectancy is 81.0 years, for Indigenous Canadians it is much lower (75.1 years for First Nations; 77.0 years for Métis; and 68.5 years for Inuit).

Using area-based analyses, Statistics Canada reports that infant mortality rates are 3.9 times higher in areas with a higher concentration of Inuit Canadians (13.5/1000 live birth); 2.3 times higher in areas with more First Nations people (8.1/1000); and 1.9 times higher in areas with more Métis people (6.6/1000) than areas with low concentrations of Indigenous people (3.5/1000). The rates of infectious and chronic diseases are also much higher in the Indigenous population in Canada. Suicide rates are five to six times higher than in the non-Indigenous population.

Rates of infectious diseases are higher for tuberculosis, pertussis, rubella, shigellosis, and chlamydia; and the tuberculosis rate among Indigenous peoples in Canada is more than five times the rate for the Canadian population as a whole. All of these afflictions are related to the problematic social determinants of health to which Indigenous peoples are exposed due to either off- or on-reserve effects of poverty.

The United Nations Declaration of the Rights of Indigenous Peoples, approved by the UN General Assembly in 2007, and signed by Canada, identifies numerous areas in which national governments could work to improve the situation of Indigenous peoples. The Declaration includes articles concerned with improving economic and social conditions; the right to attain the highest levels of health; and the right to protect and conserve their environments.

The Canadian government modified the United Nations Human Development Index (HDI) to create a Community Well-being Index (CWBI). Figure 15.1 shows how Indigenous peoples lag well behind non-Indigenous Canadians on key components of the CWBI. In 2001, using the original HDI, Canada's Indigenous peoples were ranked 33rd as a separate nation in the world community. It has been argued that Canada's Indigenous peoples now rank between 63rd and 78th on the HDI as compared to other nations.

Policy Implications

The 1996 Royal Commission on Aboriginal Peoples made a number of recommendations, virtually all of which have not been implemented.

• Recognition of an Aboriginal order of government with authority over matters related to the good government and welfare of Aboriginal peoples and their territories.

• Replacement of the federal Department of Indian Affairs with two departments, one to implement a new relationship with Aboriginal nations and one to provide services for non-self-governing communities.

• Creation of an Aboriginal Parliament.

• Initiatives to address social, education, health, and housing needs, including the training of 10,000 health professionals over a 10-year period, the establishment of an Aboriginal peoples' university, and recognition of Aboriginal nations' authority over child welfare.

And in 2015, the 2015 Truth and Reconciliation Commission released Calls to Action which contains 94 recommendations. Among these are two that take a broad approach to improving Indigenous peoples lives:

• We call upon federal, provincial, territorial, and municipal governments to fully adopt and implement the United Nations Declaration on the Rights of Indigenous Peoples as the framework for reconciliation.

• We call upon the Government of Canada to develop a national action plan, strategies, and other concrete measures to achieve the goals of the United Nations Declaration on the Rights of Indigenous Peoples.

Key sources

Assembly of First Nations (2019). Honouring Promises. 2019 Election Priorities for First Nations and Canada. Ottawa: Author.

Indigenous Services Canada (2019). Report on Trends in First Nations Communities, 1981 to 2016. Ottawa: Author. Available at https://www.sac-isc.gc.ca/eng/1345816651029/1557323327644

Royal Commission on Aboriginal Peoples. (1996). Report of the Royal Commission on Aboriginal Peoples. Ottawa: Indian and Northern Affairs.

Smiley, J. & Firestone, M. (2016). The health of Indigenous peoples. In D. Raphael (Ed.), Social Determinants of Health: Canadian Perspectives (pp. 434-466). 3rd edition. Toronto: Canadian Scholars' Press.

Truth and Reconciliation Commission of Canada (TRCC). (2015). Calls to Action. Winnipeg: TRCC. Available at: https://nctr.ca/assets/reports/Calls_to_Action_English2.pdf

United Nations (2007). The Declaration on the Rights of Indigenous Peoples. Available at https://www.un.org/esa/socdev/unpfii/documents/DRIPS_en.pdf

Figure 15.1 Average Community Well-Being Scores across First Nations and Non-Indigenous Communities, 1981 to 2016

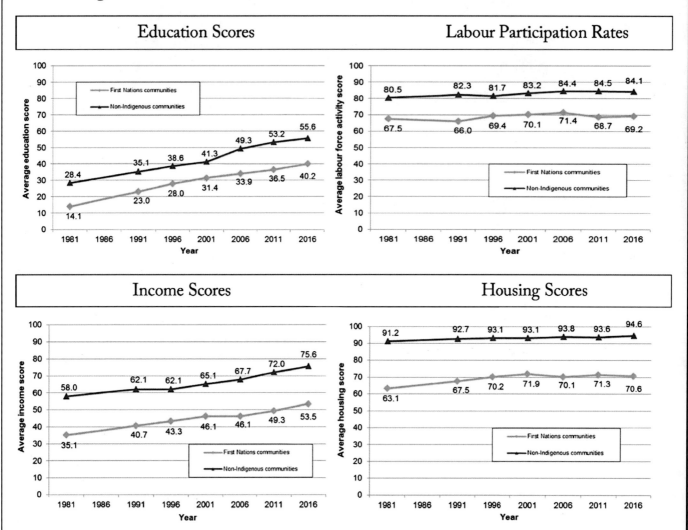

Source: Indigenous Services Canada (2019). Report on Trends in First Nations Communities, 1981 to 2016. Ottawa: Author. Available at https://www.sac-isc.gc.ca/eng/1345816651029/1557323327644

16. GENDER

Gender matters in health and care. The point may seem obvious, but it has only recently been acknowledged in health policy and research.

– Pat Armstrong, 2016

Why Is It Important?

Women in Canada experience more adverse social determinants of health than men. The main reasons for this are the consequences associated with women carrying more responsibilities for raising children and housework and systematic discrimination. Women are employed in lower paying occupations and experience more discrimination in the workplace than men. Women are also less likely than men to be working full-time and therefore less likely to be eligible for unemployment benefits when they are needed. For these reasons, almost every public policy decision that degrades employment and working conditions and the social safety net has a greater impact on women than men.

Women tend to earn less than men regardless of occupation. Women work fewer hours than men and their hourly wages are only 87 percent of the wages of men. These differences are apparent for all including those working full time/full year. This is also the case for those working full time/full year with university degrees.

Jobs which are dominated by men usually pay more, and even when women work in these fields, they are likely to get paid less. Among senior managers for example, women get paid 86 percent what men get and among top executives, the figure is only 68 percent. While the wage gap is declining, it is still significant with men earning on average

$31.05 and women, $26.92. Figure 16.1 shows the wage gap in hourly earnings by gender by province. Gaps ranged from 7.4 percent in New Brunswick to 18.6 percent in British Columbia. There was no statistically significant gender gap in hourly wages in Prince Edward Island.

International comparisons show that Canada is among the nations with the greatest gap between men and women's earnings at 18.5 percent with Canada ranking 23rd of 27 OECD nations for which data are available (Figure 16.2). Combatting discrimination in the workplace would eliminate various forms of gender-based discrimination. The gap between Canadian men's and women's wages is smaller and the provision of benefits more generous in workplaces that are unionized.

In Canada, the other major concern reflecting gender inequality is the lack of affordable and high-quality daycare. This forces many women to stay at home more and take care of family responsibilities. Making affordable childcare available would increase women's possibilities to participate in working life. Single mothers are especially at high risk of entering poverty because of the lack of affordable childcare services and women's generally lower wages.

Women have a life expectancy of 84 years as compared to men's 79.9 years. However, the higher mortality rate and lower life expectancy of men does not mean that women enjoy superior health. Women have more episodes of long-term disability and chronic diseases than men. On the other hand, men are more prone to accidents and extreme forms of social exclusion such as homelessness and severe substance abuse which reduce their overall life expectancy.

There are specific aspects of gender that pertain to men's health. The suicide rate of men is four times higher than that of women. Men are also more likely to be perpetrators and victims of robbery and physical assault. About 95 percent of Canada's prison population are men.

Young males who experience disadvantage – in the forms of poverty, low educational attainment and unemployment – are more prone to anti-social behaviours and criminal offences than women. Moreover, men's health is sometimes influenced – for the worse – by unhealthy constructs of masculinity that idealize aggressiveness, dominance and excessive self-reliance.

There is also evidence that gay, lesbian, and transgendered Canadians experience discrimination that leads to stress that has adverse health effects. This is especially a problem during adolescence when gay and lesbian youth need to come to terms with their self-identity. Discrimination is also an ongoing problem when these Canadians enter the work world.

The health of both genders is shaped by the distribution of social and economic resources. Changing these distributions requires action that extends beyond the health care or community services sectors. Required actions include the provision of living wages and adequate social assistance benefits, affordable housing and childcare, and making it easier to qualify for employment insurance. Creation and enforcement of pay equity legislation and enforcement of anti-discrimination rules are essential.

Policy Implications

• Improving and enforcing pay equity legislation would improve the employment and economic situation of Canadian women.

• Reducing the most extreme forms of poverty and social exclusion would reduce the incidence of incarceration, homelessness and severe substance abuse use among vulnerable men.

• Providing a national affordable high-quality childcare program would provide opportunities for women to engage in the workplace and improve their financial situations.

• Improving access to employment insurance for part-time workers would assist women who combine work and caregiving responsibilities.

• Creating policies that make it easier for workplaces to achieve collective agreements through unionization would be especially beneficial for Canadian women.

Key sources

Armstrong, P. (2016). Public policy, gender, and health. In D. Raphael (Ed.), Social Determinants of Health: Canadian Perspectives, 3rd edition (pp. 544-560). Toronto: Canadian Scholars' Press.

MacDonald, D. (2019). The Double-Pane Glass Ceiling: The Gender Pay Gap at The Top of Corporate Canada. Ottawa: Canadian Centre for Policy Alternatives.

Pederson, A., Raphael, D., & Johnson, E. (2019). Shifting vulnerabilities: Gender, ethnicity/race and health inequities in Canada. In T. Bryant, D. Raphael & M. Rioux (Eds.), Staying Alive: Critical Perspectives on Health, Illness, and Health Care, 3rd edition (pp. 189-232). Toronto: Canadian Scholars' Press.

Pelletier, R., Patterson, M., & Moyser, M. (2019). The Gender Wage Gap in Canada: 1998 to 2018. Ottawa: Statistics Canada. Available at https://www150.statcan.gc.ca/n1/en/pub/75-004-m/75-004-m2019004-eng.pdf?st=R2f8n885.

Scott-Samuel, A., Stanistreet, D., & Cranshaw, P. (2009). Hegemonic masculinity, structural violence and health inequalities. Critical Public Health, 19, 287-292.

Figure 16.1 Gender Wage Gap, Canadian Provinces, 2018

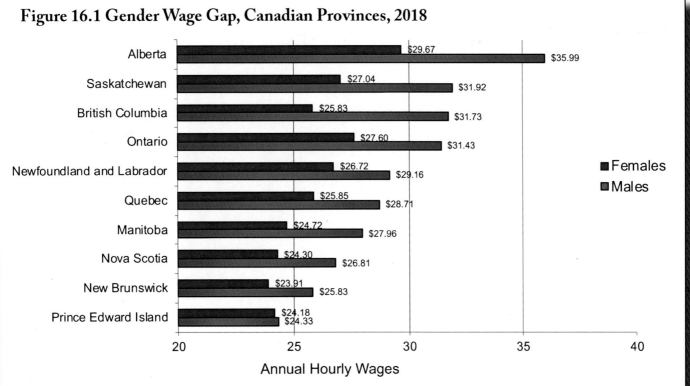

Source: Public Health Agency of Canada and Pan-Canadian Public Health Network. (2018). Key Health Inequalities in Canada: A National Portrait. Ottawa: Author.

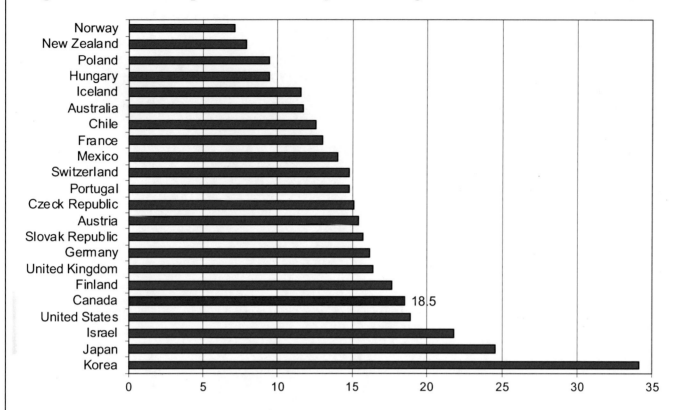

Figure 16.2 Gender Gap in Full-Time Wages, Percentage Difference, OECD Nations, 2018

Gender Wage Gap in Percentage

Source: Organisation for Economic Co-operation and Development (2020). Gender wage gap.
Available at https://data.oecd.org/earnwage/gender-wage-gap.htm

17. IMMIGRATION

Although immigration and immigrant populations have become increasingly important foci in public health research and practice, a social determinants of health approach has seldom been applied in this area. Global patterns of morbidity and mortality follow inequities rooted in societal, political, and economic conditions produced and reproduced by social structures, policies, and institutions

– Castañeda et al., 2015

Why Is It Important?

In Canada, immigration is an important source of economic growth and sociocultural diversity. According to the 2016 census, 21.9 percent of the Canadian population identify themselves as immigrants (landed immigrants, permanent residents, or naturalized citizens), with 3.5 percent of Canadians (1,212,075 individuals) being recent immigrants arriving between 2011 and 2016. Approximately 60 percent of recent immigrants qualify to enter Canada in the economic class category (professionals, skilled workers, and skilled trades) and are expected to contribute to the country's economic growth through their employment and entrepreneurship. A further 26.8 percent enter Canada as family class immigrants to join family already in Canada, and 11.6 percent arrive as refugees.

Historically, immigration to Canada was limited to those of European descent. However, with the adoption of Multiculturalism as Canadian public policy in 1971 and its inclusion in the Canadian Charter of Rights and Freedoms in 1982, most immigrants to Canada came to be non-European in origin. At present, one fifth of the Canadian population identifies as a visible minority, and this number is expected to increase significantly over the coming decades.

Being an immigrant should not predispose one to problematic living and working conditions and subsequent adverse health outcomes. However, the intersection of immigrant status with other social locations such as gender and race interact with societal conditions, shaped by public policies, to determine health. This is the case despite most immigrants to Canada being carefully selected through a point-based system based on level of education, English or French language proficiency and overall health.

Upon arrival to Canada, immigrants as a group have better health than their Canadian-born counterparts. This is explained as a result of their resourcefulness which renders them capable of relocating themselves and their families to a new country; the strict eligibility criteria that restrict immigration to those with higher immigration points; and their providing a clean bill of health prior to admittance to Canada. This observation has been described as the "healthy immigrant effect". However, despite these higher levels of health upon arrival, the health of immigrants, particularly those of non-European descent comes to decline to levels below the national average (Figure 17.1).

Non-European immigrants, especially those of colour, report higher levels of mental health problems the longer they are in Canada. These immigrants also become more likely to suffer from chronic illnesses such as adult-onset diabetes, arthritis, and heart disease.

There are several explanations for immigrants' transition to poorer health. Acculturation to a new environment and cultural norms impedes access to health care, but more importantly, immigrants' adverse health outcomes are due to a disproportionate exposure to health threatening social determinants of health that are a result of social exclusion and the racialization of poverty.

Especially important is engagement with the labour market as it the major means of securing material resources such as housing and food. Many immigrants of colour, despite having equivalent or higher educational credentials, are precariously employed – with lower wages with little or no job security – as compared to their Canadian-born counterparts.

The result of this is a higher level of poverty and material deprivation that exacerbates income and other inequalities rooted in racial discrimination, which is especially relevant as most recent immigrants are people of colour. Figure 17.2 shows that high poverty rates persist amongst Canadian immigrants even after employment is attained and these rates are higher in Canada than other nations. Not surprisingly, data from the Canadian Community Health Survey reveal that 17.1 percent of recent immigrants report being food insecure as compared to only 12.2 percent of Canadian-born individuals. One study reported levels of food insecurity as high as 64 percent in refugee families and 45 percent in recent immigrants.

In regard to core housing need, while 13 percent of Canadian households were in core housing need in 2016, 18 percent of immigrant-led households were in this situation as were 26.6 percent of recent immigrants. Food insecurity and core housing need increase vulnerability to disease during both childhood and adulthood. Adverse circumstances during childhood also leads to poor adult health.

These findings have implications for the health of Canadians. First, while all Canadians need better access to well-paying jobs, this is especially important for recent immigrants. Many immigrants lack the good working conditions that allow utilization of personal skills, thereby threatening a sense of belonging necessary for participation in various economic, social, and political aspects of Canadian life. Second, specific efforts must be made through public policies to promote the provision of economic and social security for immigrants, thereby improving the integration of immigrants into Canadian life. Third, efforts must counter increasing xenophobia and racism that threaten to exclude immigrants from the mainstream of Canadian life, thereby threatening their health and Canadian values of acceptance and tolerance.

Policy Implications

• Access to stable employment through jobs that provide adequate wages and benefits can reduce the material deprivation experienced by immigrants and promote access to opportunities over the life course to enhance health.

• Strengthening the social safety net and enhancing benefits and supports to all Canadians, especially immigrants, can enhance integration and reduce threats to health.

• Political ideologies and public discourse around immigration must deliberately counter xenophobia and racism, and greater accountability for discrimination against immigrants must be ensured at all levels of civil society.

Key sources

Canadian Mortgage and Housing Corporation (2019). Core Housing Need Data — By the Numbers. Ottawa: Author. Available at https://www.cmhc-schl.gc.ca/en/data-and-research/core-housing-need/core-housing-need-data-by-the-numbers.

Government of Canada. (2017, October 25). Immigration and Ethnocultural Diversity: Key Results from the 2016 Census. Available at http://www150.statcan.gc.ca/n1/daily-quotidien/171025/dq171025b-eng.htm?indid=14428-1&indgeo=0

Lane, V., Vatanparast, H., & White, J. (2014). Health status of newcomer children: From research to policy. In K. M. Kilbride (Ed.), Immigrant Integration: Research Implications for Future Policy (pp. 213–230). Canadian Scholars' Press Inc.

Lightman, N., & Good Gingrich, L. (2018). Measuring economic exclusion for racialized minorities, immigrants and women in Canada: Results from 2000 and 2010. Journal of Poverty, 22(5), 398–420.

Raphael, D. (2016). Immigration, Public Policy, and Health: Newcomer Experiences in Developed Nations. Toronto: Canadian Scholars' Press.

Tarasuk, V. & Mitchell A. (2020). Household Food Insecurity in Canada, 2017-18. Toronto: Research to Identify Policy Options to Reduce Food Insecurity (PROOF).

Figure 17.1 Non-European Immigrants are more likely than the Canadian-born to Report a Deterioration in Health

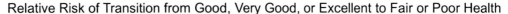
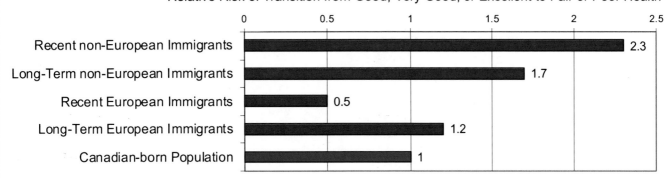

Relative Risk of Transition from Good, Very Good, or Excellent to Fair or Poor Health

Recent non-European Immigrants	2.3
Long-Term non-European Immigrants	1.7
Recent European Immigrants	0.5
Long-Term European Immigrants	1.2
Canadian-born Population	1

Source: Ng, E. et al. (2005). Healthy Today, Healthy Tomorrow? Findings from the National Population Health Survey. Ottawa: Statistics Canada.

Figure 17.2. In-Work Poverty Rates Among Native and Foreign-Born, Across Nation-Types (2012)

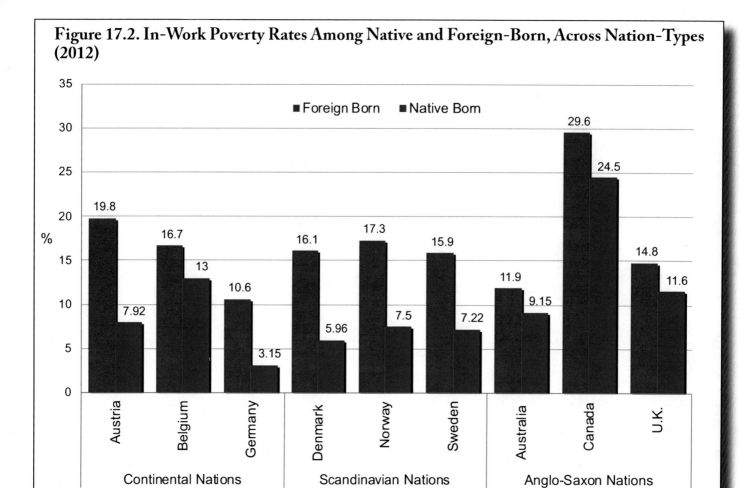

Source: Organization for Economic Cooperation and Development (2015). Settling in: OECD Indicators of Immigrant Integration 2015, Figure 1.5, p. 25). Paris: Author.

18. RACE

Research shows that racial discrimination persists in key determinant institutions such as housing, criminal justice, labour markets, education, and the health sector. That is why it is increasingly argued that racism is a social determinant of health.

– Grace-Edward Galabuzi, 2016

Why Is It Important?

Canada is a multicultural society with the ethnic and racial makeup of its population rapidly changing. In 2016, racialized Canadians made up 22 percent of the population, an increase from 16 percent in 2006. Since the 1960s over three quarters of immigrants to Canada have come from the Global South of developing nations and most are members of visible minority groups (i.e. racialized groups). The largest such groups identified in the 2016 population census are South Asians, Chinese, and Black. One third of racialized Canadians are Canadian-born with the other two-thirds immigrants. Racialized Canadians experience lower rates of income, higher rates of unemployment, and lower occupational status that threaten not only their physical, mental, and social health, but also the overall health and well-being of Canadian society.

Racism in Canadian society is responsible for these phenomena. Racism takes three forms, all of which impact health. Institutionalized racism is how racism is embedded in institutions of practice, law, and governmental inaction. Personally-mediated racism is prejudice and discrimination and manifests as lack of respect, suspicion, devaluation, scapegoating, and de-humanization. In the healthcare system, personally-mediated racism impacts quality of care for racialized persons. Internalized racism is when those who are stigmatized accept these messages about their abilities and lack of worth. This leads to resignation, helplessness, and lack of hope.

Nancy Krieger identifies six pathways by which racism harms health of which three are especially relevant to all racialized groups in Canada and the fourth for Indigenous peoples. Canada: 1) economic and social deprivation; 2) socially inflicted trauma (mental physical, and sexual, directly experienced or witnessed, from verbal threats to violent acts); 3) inadequate or degrading medical care and 4) degradation of ecosystems.

Racialized Canadians across Canada experience lower labour participation rates and higher unemployment, as well as lower incomes than Canadians of European descent (Figure 18.1). This was less so in the 1970s when their employment levels and earned incomes were similar to Canadians of European descent.

These issues apply to all racialized Canadians but their applications to Black Canadians is especially profound. While the overall proportion of Canadians obtaining post-secondary education has increased since 2011, the proportion of Black men with post-secondary education has declined.

Young Black people report experiences of racism and unfair treatment at work and are less represented at management levels and in profession such as lawyers, doctors, social workers, nurse managers, and university and college teachers.

Black Canadians experience more everyday discrimination (30.8 percent), than East/Southeast Asians (28.1 percent), South Asian/West Asians/Arabs (20.9 percent), Aboriginals (14.6 percent) and other racialized groups. Racialized Canadians report being treated with less courtesy or respect, receiving poorer services than others, treated as not smart, and perceive their presence is a threat to others.

Race is an important predictor of incarceration. Canadians who identify as Black form two percent of the population, yet compose 6 percent of the federally incarcerated. Indigenous people are approximately three percent of the population but form 24 percent of those in provincially/territorially sentenced custody.

Race is therefore a social determinant of health. Socioeconomic inequalities between racial groups explain inequalities in overall self-rated health and a wide range of physical and mental health problems. In Canada, people at risk for mental health problems are Blacks, immigrants, Latinos and Indigenous population, many of whom report anxiety about insecure and unpredictable living condition, perceived lack of control, disregard for their culture, discrimination based on multiple minority identities, and traumatic relationship with those in authority. As well, racialized Canadian immigrants are reluctant to seek medical and judicial services for fear of being treated differently or not being understood. Studies suggests that the social forces that drive racial mental health inequities result from historical legacies of social oppression.
Despite these findings, Environics Institute find that eight in ten Canadians, 84 percent of which were white, and 69 percent of Indigenous Canadians report that race relations within their communities are generally good. This contrasts with one out of every five Canadians recognizing that they often face racism with numbers rising to 50 percent for Black and Indigenous respondents. This represents a denial on the part of many Canadians that racism is a challenge in Canadian society with adverse health effects. A comprehensive strategy to combat racism is needed (Figure 18.2).

Policy Implications

• Canadians institutions must recognize the existence of racism in Canada and develop awareness and education programs that outline the adverse effects of racism.

• Governments must commit funding to enact and enforce anti-discrimination laws and regulations.

• Since people of colour are experiencing especially adverse living circumstances, governments must take an active role in improving their living and working conditions.

Key sources

Colour of Poverty-Colour of Change (2019). Fact Sheets. Toronto: Author. Available at https://colourofpoverty.ca/wp-content/uploads/2019/03/cop-coc-fact-sheet-1-about-colour-of-poverty-colour-of-change-2.pdf

Gupta, T. D., James, C. E., Andersen, C., Galabuzi, G.-E., & Maaka, R. C. (Eds.). (2018). Race and Racialization: Essential Readings (2nd ed.). Toronto: Canadian Scholars' Press.

Environics Institute (2019). Race Relations in Canada 2019 Survey. Toronto: Author.
Available at https://www.environicsinstitute.org/projects/project-details/race-relations-in-canada-2019

Hyman I., et al. (2019). Prevalence and Predictors of Everyday Discrimination in Canada: Findings from the Canadian Community Health Survey. Toronto: Wellesley Institute. Available at https://www.wellesleyinstitute.com/publications/prevalence-and-predictors-of-everyday-discrimination-in-canada-findings-from-the-canadian-community-health-survey/

Jones, C. (2000). Levels of racism: A theoretic framework and a gardener's tale. American Journal of Public Health, 90(8), 1212-1215.

Nestel, S. (2012). Colour Coded Health Care: The Impact of Race and Racism on Canadians' Health. Toronto: Wellesley Institute. Available at https://www.wellesleyinstitute.com/wp-content/uploads/2012/02/Colour-Coded-Health-Care-Sheryl-Nestel.pdf

Figure 18.1 Participation Rate, Unemployment Rate, Total Median Income and Poverty Rate (LIM-AT) for Non-Racialized and Racialized Canadians, 2015

	Participation Rate (Employed/Looking for Work) (%)	Unemployment Rate (%)	Total Median Income ($)	Poverty Rate (%)
Non-Racialized Canadians	66.5	7.3	36,538	12.2
Racialized Canadians	64.8	9.2	25,514	20.8
Arab	61.1	13.5	20,803	36.2
Black	69.0	12.5	27,263	23.9
Chinese	59.4	7.9	22,973	23.4
Filipino	77.5	5.2	32,508	7.4
Japanese	62.4	6.4	32,200	12.9
Korean	60.9	8.4	18,795	32.6
Latin American	72.7	9.1	26,843	19.8
South Asian	67.1	9.2	25,280	16.5
Southeast Asian	68.2	8.2	25,048	17.6
West Asian	63.1	11.0	19,107	17.6
All Canadians	65.2	7.7	34,025	14.2

Source: Statistics Canada (2019). Data tables, 2016 Census. Ottawa: Author.

Figure 18.2 Recommendations for a National Anti-Racism Strategy

As such, the government's Anti-Racism Strategy must be used to target the key areas where structural racism has done the most damage in our society. These areas include, but are not limited to:

- Racial inequities in the labour market
- Racialization of poverty
- Systemic racism in the criminal justice system and access to justice
- Systemic racism in national security
- Systemic racism in child welfare
- Systemic racism in health care and health inequities
- Inequities in access to basic necessities including housing and other social benefits
- Inequities in access to education, and in education outcomes
- Systemic racism in immigration legislation and policy, including temporary immigration and the interdiction regime
- Systemic racism in citizenship legislation and policy
- Hate crimes

Source: Colour of Poverty (2019). Proposed Framework for a New Anti-Racism Strategy for Canada. Toronto: Author.

19. GLOBALIZATION

The current path of globalization must change. Too few share in its benefits. Too many have no voice in its design and no influence on its course.

– Commission on the Social Dimension of Globalization, 2002

Why Is It Important?

Globalization is not a new phenomenon. Indeed, one could consider it a defining quality of so-called civilized societies if we take account of the rise and fall of empires, Europe's worldwide colonizing pursuits, and even the doctrine of 'manifest destiny' promulgated by a young USA nation in which it became white settlers' mission to shape all of North America in their image. Even measured by trade flows and international economic linkages, nations of late 19th century Europe were as highly interconnected then as now, until recessions and fierce nationalisms became the fodder for the First World War.

It was not until the 1990s, however, that the term, globalization, gained political and scholarly currency. Labonté and Torgerson succinctly define globalization as the amalgam of: "Processes by which nations, businesses, and people are becoming more connected and interdependent via increased economic integration and communication exchange, cultural diffusion […] and travel."

The emphasis here is on processes; globalization (past or present) doesn't just happen. It is a continually unfolding outcome of policies, politics, and power relations that bind nations together economically, and in turn (and through technological innovations) affects how we perceive time (everything is faster), space (the world as a global village), and ourselves (no longer just national but also 'global citizens'). But such perceptions remain the prerogative of the globally privileged, with much of our planetary fellow travelers still stranded in poverty, ill health, and worsening ecological conditions.

At base, what allows some people (and some nations) to remain healthier and wealthier and others to fail to rise much above the metrics of extreme poverty are economic transformations that began in the late 1970s with the rise of neoliberalism. Neoliberalism, an extreme form of classical liberalism that arose with capitalism in the 18th century, is a theory of political economy that emphasizes free markets, trade and finance liberalization, and minimal state governance. It came to dominate politics and forge a more globally integrated economy through three successive waves:

• A 'roll-back' of state welfare or social protection provisions as loan conditions (structural adjustment) foisted upon on indebted developing countries by the IMF and World Bank in the 1980s;

• A 'roll-out' in the form of liberalized and deregulated global finance in the 1990s that allowed multiple new ways for investors to speculate and 'game' the global economy, leading eventually to the 2008 global financial crisis and;

• A subsequent and globally-diffused imposition or voluntary acceptance of fiscal austerity to reduce government deficits primarily created by bailing out the banks and investors responsible for the 2008 crisis.

Each wave of neoliberalism has been accompanied by unequally distributed health shocks within and between countries.

Neoliberalism's 'roll back' wave had another element as well: the coerced opening of countries' economies through trade and financial liberalization, one of globalization's defining features. Economic liberalization was further cemented in place with the birth of the World Trade Organization in 1995 and a proliferation of subsequent bilateral and regional trade and investment treaties. Not that a world of protectionist nations is a healthy one; protectionism tends to breed international conflict and war. But trade and investment liberalization rules have so far disproportionately benefited wealthier people within wealthier countries largely at the expense of the rest.

Since the rise of neoliberal globalization in the 1970s income and wealth inequalities have skyrocketed to such an extent that OXFAM estimates that richest 26 billionaires now have as much wealth (and the political power it brings) as the bottom half (3.8 billion) of humanity. Since the 1980s tax rates worldwide (on corporations, high-income earners) have fallen, reducing government abilities to reduce inequalities through public programs and health-promoting investments. Labour income as a proportion of global economic activity has declined precipitously, with most of the financial gains of the past four globalizing decades going to the top 1 percent of the world's population.

Unfettered plundering of the world's ecological resources is creating climate change crises, mass species extinction, and the collapse of ecosystems essential to sustaining life. Most of this plundering has benefited the world's wealthy, while the harmful health consequences are almost entirely borne by the poor (Figure 19.1). Persisting and gross wealth inequalities, entrenched poverty, and climate change stresses (drought, famine, and floods) are driving mass migration and new forms of xenophobic and nationalist protectionist responses.

Still, there are aspects of globalization that offer some potential for reversing such toxic trends. Despite the proliferation of 'fake news' and internet trolling, digital communication and social media can create new platforms to link together community activism at local levels, with social movement activism at global scales. Sharing health knowledge across borders creates opportunities for more equitable health gains, as it did with the diffusion of low-cost health technologies (oral rehydration, promotion of breast-feeding, immunization) that led to the 'child health revolution' of the 1990s, dramatically reducing infant mortality rates.

Intergovernmental agreements through the UN and its different agencies has brought us human rights treaties, the post-2015 Sustainable Development Goals, the Paris Accord on Climate Change, and specific health treaties such as the Framework Convention on Tobacco Control. There is renewed advocacy to regulate the 'commercial determinants of (ill) health,' and to create binding and enforceable agreements to eliminate tax evasion, regulate transnational corporations, and ensure that trade treaties do not imperil health.

Contemporary globalization, by re-shaping economic and political rules, has constrained the abilities of governments and communities to create the living conditions that determine health.

But globalization's rules (and its multiple processes) are not inflexible. They can be changed. And harnessing globalization's forces for a 'health for all' is perhaps public health's greatest challenge.

Policy Implications

Re-Regulate Finance, Up to and including Bank Nationalizations:
- Restore rules that separate commercial from investment banking
- Restrict investment bankers from engaging in speculative investing on their own behalf ('proprietary trading')
- Incorporate regulatory oversight of all derivative and shadow banking transactions

Reject Austerity (fiscal contraction of government expenditures):
- Challenge neoliberal economic policies on empirical, theoretical, and ethical grounds
- Subject all new trade and investment treaties to health equity impact assessments as they are being negotiated (transparency)
- Increase public investments in public goods (creates employment, reduces inequalities, and provides needed goods and services)

Increase Progressive Taxation (increase corporate taxes, marginal income tax rates, capital gains, and impose a wealth tax):
- Close loopholes allowing tax evasion/avoidance (see Figure 19.2)
- Close offshore financial centers (tax havens)
- Support global tax reform measures (financial transaction taxes)

Key sources

Gleeson, D., & Labonté, R. (2020). Trade Agreements and Public Health: A Primer for Health Policy Makers, Researchers and Advocates. New York: Palgrave.

Labonté, R. and Ruckert, A. (2019). Health Equity in a Globalizing Era: Past Challenges, Future Prospects. Oxford: Oxford University Press.

Labonté, R., Schrecker, T., Packer, C., and Runnels, V. (Eds). (2009). Globalization and Health: Pathways, Evidence and Policy. London: Routledge.

Labonté, R., & Stuckler, D. (2016). The rise of neoliberalism: How bad economics imperils health and what to do about it. Journal of Epidemiology and Community Health, 70(3), 312-318.

Labonté, R. and Torgerson, R. (2005). Interrogating globalization, health and development: Towards a comprehensive framework for research, policy and political action. Critical Public Health 15(2), 157-179.

World Inequality Lab (2018). World Inequality Report, 2018. Paris: Paris School of Economics. Available at https://wir2018.wid.world/files/download/wir2018-full-report-english.pdf

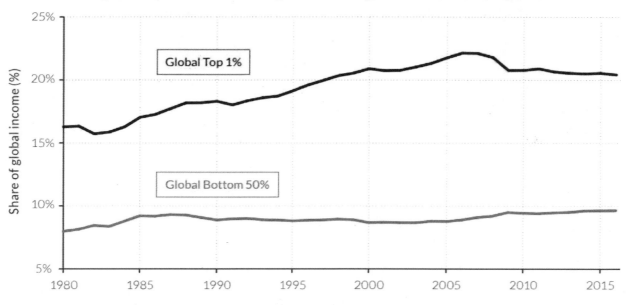

Figure 19.1 The Growth of Income Inequality during the Era of Globalization

The rise of the global top 1% versus the stagnation of the global bottom 50%, 1980–2016

Source: WID.world (2017). See wir2018.wid.world for data series and notes.

In 2016, 20% of global income was received by the Top 1% against 10% for the Bottom 50%. In 1980, 16% of global income was received by the Top 1% against 8% for the Bottom 50%.

Source: World Inequality Lab (2018). World Inequality Report, 2018. Paris: Paris School of Economics, p. 13. Available at https://wir2018.wid.world/files/download/wir2018-full-report-english.pdf

Figure 19.2 Growth in Untaxed Wealth, 2002-2016

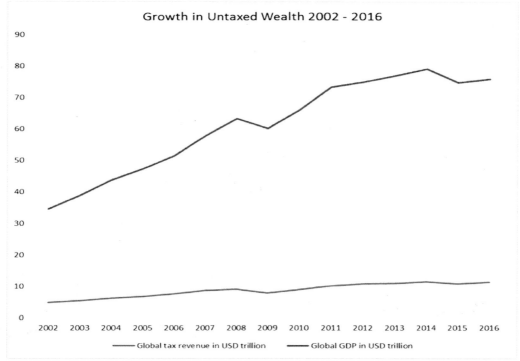

Source: Labonte, R. and Ruckert, A. (2019). Health Equity in a Globalizing Era: Past Challenges, Future Prospects, p. 395. Oxford: Oxford University Press.

20. WHAT YOU CAN DO

When a child is about to be run down by a car one pulls it on to the pavement. Not just the kindly man does that, to whom they put up monuments. Anyone pulls the child away from the car. But here many have been run down, and many pass by and do nothing.

– Bertolt Brecht, 1938

The primary means of promoting the health of Canadians is through enactment of public policies that provide the living and working conditions necessary for good health. Public policies that would improve the quality of the social determinants of health and make their distribution more equitable are not pipe dreams: they have been implemented in many wealthy nations – most of which are not as rich as Canada – to good effect. Not only can we look to other nations that apply a social determinants of health perspective, we can look to the time from the Great Depression to the period after World War II when Canada implemented Medicare and public pensions, unemployment insurance, and federal and provincial programs that delivered affordable housing, employment training, and other supports and benefits that made food banks and homeless shelters unnecessary.

Canada is now a social determinants of health laggard. Governments at all levels continue to neglect the factors necessary for health. Living and working conditions for many are not improving and are actually worsening. Since elected representatives and policymakers are aware of these problems, yet choose not to act, we must literally force them to enact health-supporting public policy. How can we do so?

In 2010, the first edition of The Canadian Facts suggested educating Canadians about the social determinants of health and asking their elected representatives what is being done to address these issues. We called for Canadians to raise these issues with agencies, organizations, and institutions whose mandates include promoting health and preventing illness such as public health units, disease associations such as Heart and Stroke Canada, Canadian Cancer Society, and Diabetes Canada. We stated health care organizations such as hospitals and professional associations should educate themselves and step-up by urging governments and policymakers to implement health promoting public policies.

There certainly has been progress in disseminating the concepts contained in the Canadian Facts. In fact, the first edition has been downloaded over one million times since 2010 with 85 percent of these downloads taking place in Canada. It has also accumulated close to 1,000 Google Scholar citations. As a result, these ideas are now commonly acknowledged by the public health and health care communities and just about every agency concerned with improving the living and working conditions of Canadians (Figure 20.1). There has been virtually no penetration of these ideas, however, amongst the major chronic disease associations in Canada. This is very troubling as it is in chronic disease morbidity and mortality during adulthood where the social determinants of health

– especially those experienced during childhood – play their greatest role.

The Canadians Facts suggested that another way to improve the quality and equitable distribution of the social determinants of health was to support political parties that were either a) receptive to the social determinants of health concept and/or b) committed to public policies that would improve their quality and equitable distribution. At that time (April 2010), it appeared that the Liberal Party and the New Democratic Party would be the parties of choice as these ideas were touched upon by candidates of both parties. This expectation evaporated during the period 2010-2020 as these parties said little about the social determinants of health. This neglect cannot be allowed to stand; citizens need to speak up to these politicians and demand serious attention to these issues.

Another way to improve the quality and equitable distribution of the social determinants of health is to strengthen those societal sectors with direct influence on these issues. Labour unions directly improve the living and working conditions of their members by providing higher wages, stronger benefits, and more health supporting workplace conditions. More broadly, the strength of labour unions within a nation is strongly related to the quality and distribution of the social determinants of health experienced by citizens. Figure 20.2 shows union density – or percentage of workers belonging to a union – and collective agreement coverage are strongly related to poverty rates. These factors are excellent indicators of a number of social determinants of health.

Social Democratic welfare states – Norway, Finland, Denmark, and Sweden – have the strongest unions and highest collective agreement rate and the lowest poverty rates; Liberal welfare states – UK, USA, Canada, New Zealand, and Australia

– have the opposite. The Continental European nations are interesting in that while union membership is not as high as in the social democratic nations, there is a recognition on the part of business and government of the value of providing workers with various forms of security: their collective agreement rate is high and their poverty rates fall midway between the Social Democratic and Liberal welfare states. The Epilogue expands upon this welfare state analysis.

Finally, Canadians can join and/or support organizations that work to strengthen the social determinants of health. Numerous groups direct their work upon specific social determinants of health. These groups act to educate and mobilize Canadians and can build pressures that can force governments to act. Some of these organizations and additional sources of information are provided in the Appendix on resources and supports.

Courage my friends,
'tis not too late to build a better world.

– Tommy Douglas,
Founder of Medicare in Canada

Key sources

Bryant, T. (2012). Applying the lessons from international experiences. In D. Raphael (Ed.), Tackling Health Inequalities: Lessons from International Experiences (pp. 265-287). Toronto: Canadian Scholars' Press.

Bryant, T. (2016). Addressing the social exclusion of immigrants through public policy action. In D. Raphael (Ed.) Immigration, Public Policy, and Health: Newcomer Experiences in Developed Nations (pp. 335-353). Toronto: Canadian Scholars' Press.

Bryant, T., & Raphael, D. (2020). The Politics of Health in the Canadian Welfare State. Toronto: Canadian Scholars' Press.

Langille, D. (2016). Follow the money: How business and politics define our health. In D. Raphael (Ed.), Social Determinants of Health: Canadian Perspectives (3rd ed., pp. 470-490). Toronto: Canadian Scholars' Press.

Raphael, D. & Curry-Stevens, A. (2016). Surmounting the barriers: Making action on the social determinants of health a public policy priority. In D. Raphael (Ed.) Social Determinants of Health Canadian Perspectives, 3rd edition (pp. 561-583). Toronto: Canadian Scholars' Press.

Raphael, D. (2020). Raising the volume on the social determinants of health in Canada and elsewhere. In E. McGibbon (Ed.) Oppression: A Determinant of Health, 2nd edition. Halifax: Fernwood Publishers.

Figure 20.1 An Example of a Health Promotion Campaign Acknowledging Social Determinants of Health

The most important things you need to know about *your health* may not be as obvious as you think.

Health = A rewarding job with a living wage
Little control at work, high stress, low pay, or unemployment all contribute to poor health.
Your job makes a difference.

Health = Food on the table and a place to call home
Having access to healthy, safe, and affordable food and housing is essential to being healthy.
Access to food and shelter makes a difference.

Health = Having options and opportunities
The thing that contributes most to your health is how much money you have. More money means having more opportunities to be healthy.
Money makes a difference.

Health = A good start in life
Prenatal and childhood experiences set the stage for lifelong health and well-being.
Your childhood makes a difference.

Health = Community belonging
A community that offers support, respect, and opportunities to participate helps us all be healthy.
Feeling included makes a difference.

How can you make a difference?
Action to improve the things that make
ALL of us healthy depends on ALL of our support.

Start a conversation.
Share what you know.

**To learn more, call the
Sudbury & District Health Unit
at (705) 522-9200, ext. 515
or visit www.sdhu.com.**

Make it a
Healthy
Day!
Sudbury & District Health Unit
Service de santé publique de Sudbury et du district

Figure 20.2 Union Density, Collective Agreement Coverage, and Overall Poverty Rates, Selected OECD Nations, 2017

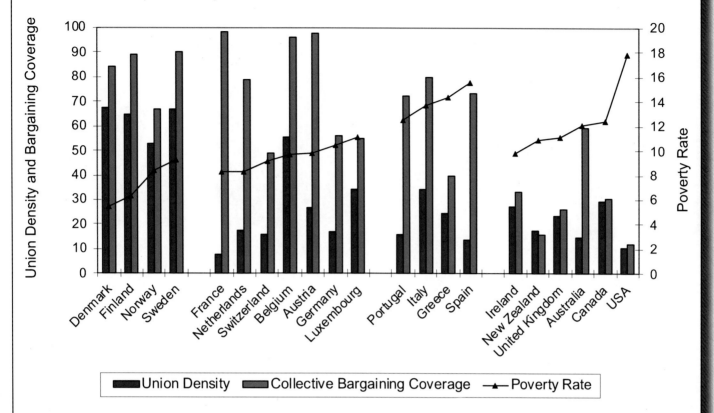

Source: Organization for Economic Cooperation and Development, trade union members and union density (2019). Available at https://stats.oecd.org/Index.aspx?DataSetCode=TUD, https://stats.oecd.org/Index.aspx?DataSetCode=TUD and Poverty Rate https://data.oecd.org/inequality/poverty-rate.htm

21. EPILOGUE

THE WELFARE STATE AND THE SOCIAL DETERMINANTS OF HEALTH

Both health, through the effects of the welfare state on the social determinants of health, and health care, through various forms of national health care systems, are tied to the fate of the welfare state.

– David Coburn, 2000

Why Is It Important?

A nation's quality and the distribution of the social determinants of health are shaped by its basket of public policies. The term welfare state has come to stand for these public policies and how they provide economic and social security to societal members. Much of what has been presented in Social Determinants of Health: The Canadian Facts can be explained by Canada being what is termed a Liberal welfare state.

Forms of the Welfare State

Gosta Esping-Andersen identified three forms of the welfare state in wealthy nations. These are the Social Democratic, Conservative and Liberal. The Social Democratic welfare states (e.g. Finland, Sweden, Denmark and Norway) emphasize universal welfare rights and provide generous entitlements and benefits. Their political and social history is one of political dominance by Social Democratic parties of the left, a result of the initial political organization of industrial workers and farmers, and later the middle class. Through universal provision of these supports, these regimes have secured the loyalties of a significant proportion of the population.

Conservative welfare states (e.g. Belgium, France, Germany and Netherlands) also offer generous benefits, but provide these through social insurance plans associated with employment rank with primary emphasis on male wage earners. Their political and social history is one of political dominance by Christian Democratic parties where traditional Catholic Church concerns with supporting citizens merged with traditional approaches towards maintaining status differences and adherence to authority. These tendencies sometimes manifest in corporatist approaches (e.g. Germany) where business interests are major influences or in Statist approaches (e.g. France) where the State plays a key role in provision of citizen security.

Liberal welfare states (e.g. Australia, Canada, Ireland, New Zealand, UK and USA) provide modest benefits. The State usually provides assistance only when the economic market fails to meet citizens' most basic needs. Their political and social history is one of dominance by corporate and business interests and Liberal political parties that has led the population to give its loyalty to the economic system rather than the State as means of providing economic and social security.

The primary aim of Liberal welfare states is to strengthen the economy. This usually translates into greater support for the advocacy positions of the corporate and business sector, which by reducing the role of the State, produces economic and social insecurity for many, if not most citizens. These Liberal welfare states are therefore the least developed in providing citizens with economic and social security. A key feature is use of means-tested benefits that target only the least well-off and are only intended to meet immediate needs.

In Canada, both the two dominant political parties, the Liberal Party and the Conservative Party, are considered by political scientists to be Liberal political parties. Both political parties have ties to the corporate and business sector and enact policies supporting their interests over those of many, if not most, Canadians. The focus is on reducing the role of the State in managing the economy (e.g., setting wages and working conditions, providing universal benefits and supports) in ways that exacerbate the economic vulnerability of women, people with disabilities, those with less education, immigrants and racialized populations among others. This greater support for the advocacy positions of the corporate and business sector produces economic and social insecurity for many if not most Canadians.

The primary aim of Liberal welfare states is therefore to strengthen the economy. Liberal welfare state politicians claim to be sympathetic to the needs of ordinary Canadians. Indeed, the Liberal government of Prime Minister Justice Trudeau has enacted income-support programs to support Canadians who have lost their jobs as a result of the COVID-19 pandemic. It has raised the possibility of 'topping up' the wages of personal support workers and others deemed essential for the duration of the pandemic. These are means of preserving the economy during the pandemic crisis.

It is unlikely, however, that these programs will continue once public health officials declare the pandemic over. Such programs are inconsistent with the ethos of Liberal welfare states that have not only minimized the role of the State in resource provision and distribution but have increasingly adopted austerity approaches to governance in support of their pro-business agenda. Austerity means even lower public expenditures, lessened taxation on corporations and the wealthy, and a smaller State role in providing economic and social security to the majority of Canadians than has traditionally been the case.

If Canada's Liberal political parties are found to be lacking, Canada does have a Social Democratic political party, the NDP, which should be amenable to promoting the social determinants of health. The USA, in contrast, does not have a viable Social Democratic party. Both the Democratic Party and the Republican Party are considered to be Liberal political parties serving primarily the interests of the corporate and business elite.

Researchers have added a fourth form of the welfare state to the three identified by Esping-Andersen. Latin welfare states (e.g. Greece, Italy, Spain and Portugal) are less developed family-oriented versions of the Conservative welfare state. However, they generally provide more supports to citizens than Liberal welfare states. These nations have been experiencing financial crises related to lower revenues as a result of the imposition of austerity policies and tax avoidance that threaten their welfare state and the income and social security of their populations. Figure 21.1 provides the distinctive features of each form of the welfare state.

The Importance of the Welfare State

But there is much more to the welfare state than the supports and benefits it provides. Welfare states also reflect how a society views what it owes to members simply by virtue of citizenship or residence. Social Democratic, Conservative, and Latin welfare states are about more than economic growth. They exist to promote equality in the case of the Social Democratic welfare state and solidarity in the case of the Conservative and Latin welfare states. This leads to distinctive patterns of State and workplace organization that ensures economic and social security to their members. In contrast, the Liberal welfare state emphasizes liberty in the economic marketplace, doing rather less to provide economic and social security to its members. This emphasis on liberty in the Liberal welfare state builds distrust in governments. This plays out in inadequate public policies in areas such as income security, employment and working conditions, health care, housing and food security, and supports to children, families, and older persons.

Research supports this typology of welfare states. When indicators of government spending and organization and distribution of benefits are subject to empirical analyses, three type or four type groupings usually emerge. Nations such as Austria and Switzerland sometimes appear as different welfare state types, but findings involving Canada, however, are unambiguous. While no less than 12 welfare state typologies have been devised, in six of the seven typologies that include Canada, it is in the group similar to the Liberal welfare state: Liberal, Basic Security, or Liberal Anglo-Saxon, the exception being for the provision of health care where Canada is grouped within the Conservative cluster. Canada is a Liberal welfare state.

This analysis identifies some of the key barriers (e.g., corporate and business influence upon public policy, citizen distrust of government, and dominance by Liberal political parties) to improving the quality and distribution of the social determinants of health in Canada. It also identifies entry points for public policy action that can improve the quality and distribution of the social determinants of health.

Canada's first-past-the-post electoral system is also a barrier to welfare state development. Proportional representation election systems are associated with more comprehensive welfare states that provide better quality and more equitable distribution of the social determinants of health. This is accomplished by the necessity of governing coalitions that include Social Democratic political parties as Liberal or Christian Democratic parties rarely achieve a majority of the seats in parliaments under proportional representation voting systems.

Welfare state analysis does not change any of the recommendations that we have presented. It does, however, place these recommendations within the context of the structures and processes of the Canadian welfare state that have, to date, made implementation of these recommendations difficult. Liberal welfare states can change. But they will do so only when the members of society demand public policy in the service of health.

Key sources

Bambra, C. (2007). Going beyond the three worlds of welfare capitalism: Regime theory and public health research. Journal of Epidemiology and Community Health, 61(12), 1098-1102.

Bryant, T., & Raphael, D. (2020). The Politics of Health in the Canadian Welfare State. Toronto: Canadian Scholars' Press.

Bryant, T., & Raphael, D. (2018). Welfare States, Public Health and Health Inequalities. Oxford: Oxford Bibliographies. Available at https://www.oxfordbibliographies.com/view/document/obo-9780199756797/obo-9780199756797-0178.xml

Esping-Andersen, G. (1990). The Three Worlds of Welfare Capitalism. Princeton: Princeton University Press.

Evans, B. M., & McBride, S. (Eds.). (2018). The Austerity State. Toronto: University of Toronto Press.

Saint-Arnaud, S., & Bernard, P. (2003). Convergence or resilience? A hierarchical cluster analysis of the welfare regimes in advanced countries. Current Sociology, 51(5), 499-527.

Figure 21.1 Ideological Variations in Forms of the Welfare State

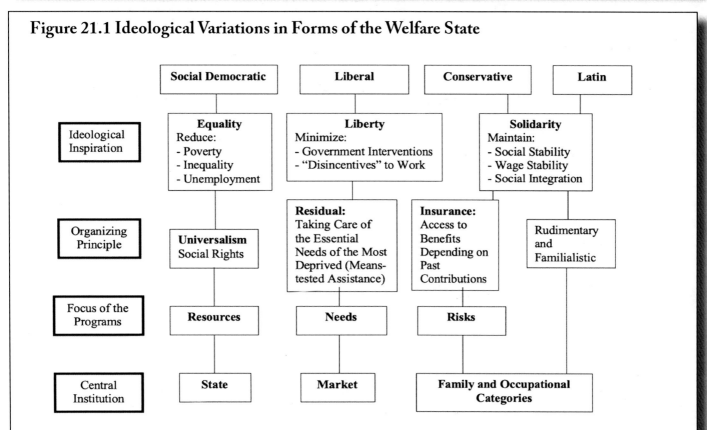

Source: Saint-Arnaud, S., and Bernard, P. (2003). Convergence or resilience? A hierarchical cluster analysis of the welfare regimes in advanced countries (Figure 2, p. 503). Current Sociology, 51(5), 499–527.

APPENDIX I. RESOURCES AND SUPPORTS

Resources on the Social Determinants of Health in Canada

Print Materials

Chronic Disease Prevention Alliance of Ontario (2008). Primer to Action: Social Determinants of Health. Toronto: Author.
– https://en.healthnexus.ca/sites/en.healthnexus.ca/files/resources/primer_to_action.pdf

Raphael, D. (2016). About Canada: Health and Illness, 2nd edition.
Halifax: Fernwood Publishers.

Raphael, D. (2016). Social Determinants of Health: Canadian Perspectives, 3rd edition.
Toronto: Canadian Scholars' Press.

World Health Organization. (2008). Closing the Gap in a Generation: Health Equity through Action on the Social Determinants of Health. Geneva: World Health Organization.
https://www.who.int/social_determinants/thecommission/finalreport/en/

Media Resources

California Newsreel (2008). Unnatural Causes: Is Inequality Making Us Sick?
– http://www.unnaturalcauses.org/

Public Health Agency of Canada (2019). Health Inequalities in Canada.
– https://www.youtube.com/watch?v=RMkBUXJLW9g&feature=youtu.be

Poor No More (2010). – http://www.poornomore.ca/

Santé Montréal (2014). Unequal - Social Inequalities in Health
– https://www.youtube.com/watch?v=u7qtRvjGPZg

Let's Start a Conversation about Health (2020).
– https://tinyurl.com/vs6fuxg

Website Resources

Canadian Public Health Association: Resources
– https://www.cpha.ca/social-determinants-health-resources

Homeless Hub – https://www.homelesshub.ca/

Research to Identify Policy Options to Reduce Food Insecurity
– https://proof.utoronto.ca/

Public Health Agency of Canada: Social Determinants of Health
– https://www.canada.ca/en/public-health/services/health-promotion/population-health/what-determines-health.html

Social Determinants of Health Communication Network
– https://listserv.yorku.ca/archives/sdoh.html

World Health Organization: Social Determinants of Health Action
– https://www.who.int/social_determinants/actionsdh/en/

Policy and Advocacy Organizations Addressing the Social Determinants of Health

Progressive Public Policy Organizations
Acorn Canada – https://acorncanada.org/
Broadbent Institute – https://www.broadbentinstitute.ca/
Canadian Centre for Policy Alternatives – http://www.policyalternatives.ca/
Council of Canadians – https://canadians.org/
Parkland Institute – https://www.parklandinstitute.ca/
Wellesley Institute – https://www.wellesleyinstitute.com/

SDOH Advocacy Organizations
Upstream – https://www.thinkupstream.net/
People's Health Movement Canada – https://phm-na.org/
Health Promotion Canada – https://www.healthpromotioncanada.ca/

Childcare
Childcare Canada Resource and Research Unit – https://www.childcarecanada.org/
Child Care Now – https://timeforchildcare.ca/

Disability Groups
Disabled Women's Network of Canada – https://www.dawncanada.net/
Council of Canadians with Disabilities – http://www.ccdonline.ca/en/
Independent Living Canada – https://www.ilc-vac.ca/

Employment and Working Conditions
Canadian Labour Congress – https://canadianlabour.ca/
Institute for Work & Health – https://www.iwh.on.ca/

Food Insecurity
Food Secure Canada – https://foodsecurecanada.org/
Dietitians of Canada: Action Groups – https://www.dietitians.ca/Advocacy/LAG-pages

Geography
Canadian Northern and Remote Health Network
– https://www.cfhi-fcass.ca/WhatWeDo/northern-remote-collaboration
Institute for Circumpolar Health Research – http://www.ichr.ca/

Globalization
Council of Canadians: Trade – https://canadians.org/trade
CCPA Trade and Investment Research Project
– https://www.policyalternatives.ca/projects/trade-and-investment-research-project

Health Services
Canadian Health Coalition – http://www.healthcoalition.ca/
Canadian Doctors for Medicare – https://www.canadiandoctorsformedicare.ca/
Health Providers Against Poverty – https://healthprovidersagainstpoverty.ca/

Housing and Homelessness
Centre for Urban and Community Studies, University of Toronto
– http://www.urbancentre.utoronto.ca/
Cooperative Housing Federation – https://chfcanada.coop/
Homeless Hub – https://www.homelesshub.ca/
Right to Housing – https://righttohousing.wordpress.com/

Indigenous Health
Assembly of First Nations – https://www.afn.ca/Home/
National Aboriginal Health Organization – http://www.naho.ca/
National Collaboration Centre on Indigenous Health – https://www.nccih.ca/en/

Immigration
Canadian Council for Refugees – https://ccrweb.ca/
KAIROS: Migrant Justice – https://www.kairoscanada.org/what-we-do/migrant-justice
Ontario Council of Agencies Serving Immigrants – https://ocasi.org/

Income
Basic Income Network Canada – https://www.basicincomecanada.org/
Canada without Poverty – http://www.cwp-csp.ca/
Campaign 2000 – https://campaign2000.ca/
Citizens for Public Justice – https://cpj.ca/
Interfaith Social Assistance Reform Coalition – https://isarc.ca/
Ontario Coalition Against Poverty – https://ocap.ca/

Race
Canadian Anti-Hate Network – https://www.antihate.ca/
The Canadian Ecumenical Anti-Racism Network – https://www.councilofchurches.ca/social-justice/undoing-racism/anti-racism-network/
Colour of Poverty – https://colourofpoverty.ca/

Social Exclusion
Maytree Foundation – https://maytree.com/
Metropolis Project – http://canada.metropolis.net/generalinfo/index_e.html

Women
CCPA Making Women Count Project
– https://www.policyalternatives.ca/projects/making-women-count
CEDAW - Feminist Alliance for International Action
– http://fafia-afai.org/en/womens-rights/cedaw/
YWCA Canada – http://www.ywcacanada.ca/

APPENDIX II. QUOTATION SOURCES

1. Introduction

Roy Romanow is a former Premier of Saskatchewan and was Commissioner of the Royal Commission on the Future of Health Care in Canada. The quotation is from his foreword to Social Determinants of Health: Canadian Perspectives, 1st edition.

2. Stress, Bodies, and Illness

Robert Evans is a Professor Emeritus at the Centre for Health Services and Policy Research at the University of British Columbia. The quotation is from the volume Why are some People Healthy and Others Not?

3. Income and Income Distribution

Andrew Jackson is Senior Policy Adviser to the Broadbent Institute. **Govind Rao** is a Senior Research Officer for the Canadian Union of Public Employees, National Office. The quotation is taken from their chapter in Social Determinants of Health: Canadian Perspectives, 3rd edition.

4. Education

Charles Ungerleider is a Professor Emeritus of Educational Studies at the University of British Columbia. **Tracey Burns** is a Project Leader in the Education Directorate of the Organisation for Economic Cooperation and Development in Paris. The quotation is taken from their chapter in Social Determinants of Health: Canadian Perspectives, 3rd edition.

5. Unemployment and Job Insecurity

Emile Tompa is senior scientist at the Institute for Work & Health in Toronto. **Michael Polanyi** is a Community Worker at the Children's Aid Society of Toronto. **Janice Foley** is an associate professor in the Faculty of Business Administration at the University of Regina. The quotation is taken from their chapter in Social Determinants of Health: Canadian Perspectives, 3rd edition.

6. Employment and Working Conditions

Peter Smith is a researcher at the Institute for Work & Health in Toronto. **Michael Polanyi** is a Community Worker at the Children's Aid Society of Toronto. The quotation is taken from their chapter in Social Determinants of Health: Canadian Perspectives, 3rd edition.

7. Early Child Development

The Federal/Provincial Territorial Advisory Committee on Population Health is responsible for advising governments on health policy and related issues. The quotation is from its 1996 Report on the Health of Canadians.

8. Food Insecurity

Lynn McIntyre is Professor Emerita of in the Department of Community Health Sciences at the University of Calgary. **Krista Rondeau** is a research and evaluation consultant in primary care and food insecurity. The quotation is taken from their chapter in Social Determinants of Health: Canadian Perspectives, 2nd edition.

9. Housing

Toba Bryant is an associate professor in the Faculty of Health Sciences at Ontario Tech University in Oshawa, Ontario. The quotation is taken from her chapter in Social Determinants of Health: Canadian Perspectives, 3rd edition.

10. Social Exclusion

Grace-Edward Galabuzi is an associate professor at Ryerson University in the Department of Politics and Public Administration. The quotation is taken from his chapter in Social Determinants of Health: Canadian Perspectives, 3rd edition.

11. Social Safety Net

David Langille teaches Health Policy at the University of Toronto and York University and is the executive producer of the film Poor no More. The quotation is taken from his chapter in Social Determinants of Health: Canadian Perspectives, 3rd edition.

12. Health Services

Elizabeth McGibbon is a professor of nursing at St. Francis Xavier University. The quotation is taken from her chapter in Social Determinants of Health: Canadian Perspectives, 3rd edition.

13. Geography

Trevor Dummer is an associate professor in the School of Population and Public Health at the University of British Columbia. The quotation is from the article Health Geography: Supporting Public Health Policy and Planning published in the Canadian Medical Association Journal.

14. Disability

Marcia Rioux is a Professor Emerita at the School of Health Policy and Management at York University. **Tamara Daly** is a professor in the School of Health Policy and Management at York University. The quotation is taken from their chapter in Staying Alive: Critical Perspectives on Health, Illness, and Health Care, 3rd edition.

15. Indigenous Ancestry

Janet Smylie is a physician and research scientist at the Centre for Research on Inner City Health and associate professor in the Department of Public Health Sciences at the University of Toronto. **Michelle Firestone** is a Scientist at the Well Living House in the Centre for Urban Health Solutions of St. Michael's Hospital. The quotation is taken from their chapter in Social Determinants of Health: Canadian Perspectives, 3rd edition.

16. Gender

Pat Armstrong is Distinguished Research Professor of Sociology at York University. The quotation is taken from her chapter in Social Determinants of Health: Canadian Perspectives, 3rd edition.

17. Immigration

Heide Castañeda is in the Department of Anthropology, University of South Florida. The quotation is from the article Immigration as a Social Determinant of Health in the Annual Review of Public Health.

18. Race

Grace-Edward Galabuzi is an associate professor at Ryerson University in the Department of Politics and Public Administration. The quotation is taken from his chapter in Social Determinants of Health: Canadian Perspectives, 3rd edition.

19. Globalization

The World Commission on the Social Dimension of Globalization was initiated by the International Labour Organization to respond to the needs of people as they cope with the unprecedented changes that globalization has brought to their lives, families, and societies in which they live. The quotation is from Globalization for People: A Vision for Change.

20. What You Can Do

Bertolt Brecht was a German theatre practitioner, playwright, and poet who came to be one of the most prominent figures in 20th-century theatre. The quotation is from his poem The World's One Hope.

21. Epilogue: The Welfare State and the Social Determinants of Health

David Coburn is Professor Emeritus at the University of Toronto. The quotation is from his article Income Inequality, Social Cohesion and Health Status of Populations: The Role of Neo-Liberalism, published in Social Science and Medicine.

Manufactured by Amazon.ca
Acheson, AB

11002501R00057